'TO THINE O[WN SELF BE TRUE]'
A GUIDE TO ASSERTIVENESS IN THE WORKPLACE

SUE HOLMES

ASSET BOOKS LTD., DORKING, SURREY RH4 2TU, UNITED KINGDOM

©1995 Asset Books Ltd,
1 Paper Mews, 330 High Street,
Dorking, Surrey RH4 2TU.

All rights reserved.

No part of this publication may be reproduced, stored in a retrieval system, or transmitted in any form or by any means, electronic, mechanical, photocopying, recording or otherwise without the written permission of the copyright holders. This book may not be sold, lent, hired out or otherwise dealt with in the course of trade of supply in any form of binding other than that in which it is published without the prior permission of the publishers.

A catalogue record for this book is available from the British Library.

ISBN 1 900179 02 4

Printed and bound in Great Britain by Prisma Press

CONTENTS

Chapter 1: WHAT IS ASSERTIVENESS? — 1
   Assertion — 1
   Non-assertion — 2
      Aggression — 2
      Passivity — 3
      Manipulation — 4
   Assertive behaviour — 4
   Effects of different behavioural styles — 5
   The assertive response — 7

Chapter 2: CONCEPTS OF ASSERTIVENESS — 9
   Rights and assertive behaviour — 9
   Responsibilities — 13
   Personal beliefs: their influence on acceptance of rights — 14
      Modifying your beliefs — 15

CHAPTER 3: IT AIN'T WHAT YOU DO... — 17
   Communication skills — 17
   Communication in the workplace — 22

CHAPTER 4: ...IT'S THE WAY THAT YOU DO IT — 24
   Body language — 24
      First impressions — 25
      What does your body language say about you? — 26

CHAPTER 5: CONFLICT AND DISAGREEMENT — 30
   Giving criticism — 30
   Receiving criticism — 31
   Anger — 33
      Dealing with anger in others — 37
   Managing disagreement — 37
      Constructive disagreement — 38

CHAPTER 6: FEEDBACK AND PRAISE — 40
   Giving praise — 40
   Receiving praise — 42

CHAPTER 7: SAYING NO (OR YES)	45
Refusing a request	45
The assertive way of saying no	45
Tips for assertive refusal	49
Saying 'yes'	50
Making requests	51
Negotiation and compromises	52
Reaching agreement	54
CHAPTER 8: DEALING WITH NON-ASSERTION IN OTHERS	55
Handling aggression	55
Handling passivity	57
CHAPTER 9: A PROGRAMME FOR CHANGE	60
Final tips	68
REFERENCES	70
FURTHER READING	70

CHAPTER 1: WHAT IS ASSERTIVENESS?

If you work with other people there will be times when 'difficult situations' will arise which may make you feel frustrated, anxious, angry or worried; at times they may result in confrontation or even open conflict. Commonly, we ignore such events in the hope that they will go away of their own accord. This approach can, of course, have advantages in that people can, and often do, solve their own problems while others may simply use avoiding tactics to prevent argument and disagreement. However, there are also disadvantages in that there may be high levels of frustration in individuals and a marked lack of teamwork; there may be poor communication between departments and teams, and even individuals. Working in such environments is uncomfortable and possibly stressful.

Working successfully with others is largely dependent on the relationships between those involved. Most of the time these will be harmonious but, inevitably, difficulties will arise from time to time and, regardless of the cause, must be resolved if relationships are to be maintained. It is undoubtedly true that the effectiveness of both individuals and the organisations in which individuals work, can be affected by the success with which such situations are dealt with.

The purpose of this book is to offer some solutions that could be adopted in attempting to achieve this. Its intention is to help anyone who would like to be more effective in standing up for themselves and their rights, influencing others and handling difficult people and situations. This text is designed to increase awareness of personal behaviour - and the response we get to this - and to propose an alternative behaviour and examine the responses this achieves. In this way I hope to lay the foundations for successfully modifying your behaviour and increasing your personal effectiveness.

ASSERTION

I'm sure we can all think of situations in which, despite our good intentions, our actions did not achieve the results we wanted. Assertive behaviour aims to help us overcome this problem. It deals not only with what we do but how we do it. Assertiveness literally means that we have the ability to state something clearly, honestly and directly, to acknowledge our personal feelings, needs and beliefs, and to have them both recognised and respected. In other words to be much more positive about ourselves and our views and to take responsibility for them.

Thus self-assertion recognises your rights and reflects your beliefs, needs and wants at any given time and in any given situation. This could imply that it is selfish but, since recognising your rights implicitly leads to recognition that others also have rights, this is not so. It is a reciprocal relationship, an interaction between equals based on two fundamental beliefs:

- You have rights and needs to be met; others have the same
- Both you and others have something to contribute to work and to interpersonal relationships.

Assertiveness thus aims to satisfy the needs of all involved; it is what Berne (1967) described as 'win-win' behaviour that leaves everyone feeling that they have gained something from an interaction. It is about having confidence in yourself and a positive attitude and respect for both yourself and for others.

NON-ASSERTION

Non-assertion can be seen as a failure to express yourself honestly or to make your feelings clear, so that non-assertive people often allow themselves to be taken for granted or to be 'walked over'. Although becoming assertive can help to prevent this it is important to realise that you can choose to accept non-assertion or take positive action to overcome it.

Taking responsibility for your feelings allows you to change them; failing to do so means that you transfer power to others who can make you angry or unhappy as they like. Developing assertiveness thus enables you to do something about the anger and frustration you feel. The power of choice is your ultimate freedom.

Aggression

Aggression is a non-assertive behaviour which, like assertion, involves recognising and standing up for your rights but, unlike assertion, means ignoring the rights of others and dismissing their

Table 1.1   Non-assertive behaviour
(Modified from Townend (1991, p24-25)

Those who are not assertive may display the following:

All:
Lack of self-respect or self-confidence
Low self-esteem
Negative self-image
Lack of motivation

Aggression:
Lack of respect for others
Feelings of superiority
Liking to be in control
Disinterest in others
Quick to allocate blame
Dismissive of feedback

Manipulation:
Mistrust or suspicion of other's motives
Dishonest and indirect
'Twist' what other's say
Undermine self-esteem in others

Passivity:
Self-criticism
Feelings of inferiority
Avoidance of conflict
Liking others to be in control

needs. It suggests that you put your needs first. Aggression may lead to failure to take responsibility for your actions, you may blame others who have 'driven you to it'. It may reflect insecurity and vulnerability and be mediated by anger or fear. Many aggressive people are highly competitive constantly striving to 'win', whatever the cost. In reality, this is 'no-win' behaviour reflecting shaky self-esteem and anxiety about 'what people think' while demonstrating a lack of respect for them. It is selfish and self-centred (see page 6).

Passivity

Passive people put the needs of others before their own appearing to believe that their needs are less important. They fail to stand up for their rights or do this in apologetic or self-effacing ways so that it is easy for others to overlook them. They rarely make eye contact with others, making it difficult to build a rapport, and displaying signs of discomfort.

For some, this reflects a lack of confidence in themselves or their ability and a tendency to compare themselves unfavourably with others; they invite negative recognition that confirms their negative view of themselves. Many are shy and terrified of making mistakes or looking foolish and, like those who are aggressive, often worry about what others may think. Their behaviour is, therefore, designed to avoid conflict and please others. It reflects a shaky self-esteem but it is also selfish because passive people often forget to think about how others may be feeling.

Manipulation

Manipulation reflects the actions of those achieving their objectives indirectly. It often has a short-term 'pay off' and so can be difficult to change; it can also be difficult to identify this behaviour in either yourself or others although, in the long-term, it can be disruptive to working relationships. Manipulative people usually have low self-esteem and often view others negatively. They are often depressed and demotivated lacking self-confidence and finding it difficult to trust others or themselves.

> **EXERCISE:**
> Set aside a time, 15 minutes or so, when you can be alone and list 10-12 situations at work when you would like to be more assertive. These may be, for example, times when you are unfairly criticised or asked to take on additional tasks.
> When you have completed your list, reflect on the way you behave now in response to each situation (aggressive, passive, manipulative) and make a note of this. You may find that you respond differently at different times; if so note this also.

You have probably found that you move between behavioural styles at different times and in different circumstances. This is not unusual.

ASSERTIVE BEHAVIOUR

You can now see that assertiveness is *not* about winning at all costs or getting what you want at the expense of others. Instead it reflects

Table 1.2   Assertive behaviour

> Those who are assertive are likely to display the following:
> - Self-confidence
> - High self-esteem
> - Ability to take responsibility for themselves
> - Interest in the feelings of others
> - Ability to ask questions
> - Ability to listen effectively
> - Honesty and 'directness'
> - Motivated to do a good job
> - Ability to request feedback

belief that the needs, wants and desires of others are equally important. Assertive people prioritise their needs in relation to those of others thus displaying respect for both parties (Table 1.2). Thus they will think before they speak and, although their needs are clearly stated, they do not threaten others. They will demonstrate respect and understanding of others' needs and feelings. They will be prepared to compromise, not through passivity but through choice.

EFFECTS OF DIFFERENT BEHAVIOURAL STYLES

In adopting non-assertive behaviours we deny our feelings and so act dishonestly. This is rarely a conscious act but clearly affects both ourselves and other people; it may also influence our workplace in part or in whole. An example will help to illustrate this.

Imagine the situation: Your manager has asked you to complete an extra task by the end of the week. You are clearly the best person to do this but you're heavily committed to other work. In any case, your colleagues have less work to do and you don't think this is fair. How do you feel?

You are probably resentful that your colleagues have an easy time whilst you are overloaded. Anyway, if you try to complete more work you'll be trying to do so much that none will be done properly.

You may be aggressive, saying irritably, *'Its not fair! You always expect me to do extra work. I'm not going to do that!'*. You look angry and thump the desk as you're talking. You may be passive, speaking quietly and keeping your eyes on the desk in front of you. *'Oh, I'm terribly sorry but I don't think I can. I'm already behind with my work and I've promised to do that report for John. I'm sorry'*. You feel guilty later. Alternatively you may agree, working late every night to complete it.

Neither response is desirable. Aggression leaves you feeling angry and may provoke various reactions from your manager. He may ask someone else to do the work, unsatisfactory because he wanted you to do it. Thus this solution does not meet his needs. Further, you don't appear to have respected his feelings and have blamed him for 'expecting' you to do the work.

Alternatively, he may respond angrily to your aggression pushing the work on to you. This is also unsatisfactory as it doesn't take account of your needs and leaves you feeling even more angry. Aggression has left both of you dissatisfied. It may also have damaged the relationship between you.

The effects of aggression

The immediate effects of aggression may relieve tension and allow the release of pent-up feelings. You may be pleased with the outcome as it has relieved you of additional work. This feels good. However, the long-term effects may be different. You may feel guilty or ashamed of losing your temper and become unduly apologetic or excessively helpful in attempts to reduce your embarrassment. In time you come to resent the situation and revert to aggression.

Alternatively, continuing aggression, reinforced by getting what you want, may lead you to be constantly alert and prepared to ensure that you're not 'taken advantage of'. Thus you will be constantly tense and suspicious of other's motives which leaves you tired and emotionally drained at the end of the day. In the long-term, this can leave you isolated making it difficult to sustain friendships, or cause stress or stress-related disorders (Gournay, 1995) all of which are undesirable.

The effects of passivity

Since your main aim is to avoid conflict and please your manager; you are not taking yourself or your feelings into account. His needs are more important than yours. This may make you resentful later, particularly if you have to work late. As his work will be done your manager's needs will be met although, due to your resentment, it may be of a lower quality than he (or you) would like.

Again, passivity may have some short-term benefits; potential conflict and guilt have been avoided. You may even be proud that you have 'done him a favour'. But, in the longer-term, passivity may lead to increasing loss of self-esteem as others' needs dominate. You may feel angry or frustrated and, in time, start to feel sorry for yourself. Increasingly, because you always try to avoid conflict, others will come to take your co-operation for granted. You begin to 'put yourself down' further decreasing your self-esteem. This introspection focuses heavily on your feelings, leading to tension and, again, causing stress. Yet despite its undesirable effects, passivity continues if it is reinforced by demonstrable short-term benefits.

THE ASSERTIVE RESPONSE

So how should we respond? An assertive response would express concern for your manager's position, explain your situation and make a constructive suggestion for solving the problem. You might say something like: *'I understand your problem but I can't do it this week. I could do it first thing on Monday, you could have it before 11.00'*. This would make your feelings clear and acknowledge your manager's difficulty, respecting his position and, in making a constructive suggestion, you have laid the ground for a positive outcome.

> **EXERCISE:**
> Look at the list you made earlier and identify a situation in which you behave aggressively. Reflect on this and ask yourself:
> - What are the advantages and disadvantages of behaving in this way in this situation?
> - What might you gain if you were to be assertive?
>
> Repeat the exercise looking at situations in which you behave passively.

This will help you to explore your own ideas and experiences enabling you to decide whether you want to maintain your existing behaviour or to learn to be assertive. Making a positive choice encourages positive action. Evaluating our behaviour helps us to identify the way we currently act in given situations. If we're truthful about this, we can begin to acknowledge our behaviour and to accept where we are; we can only move forward once we have done so.

CHAPTER 2: CONCEPTS OF ASSERTIVENESS

In learning to be assertive we must both understand assertion theory and practise its skills. Increased understanding and awareness of different behaviours is helpful in achieving this. As with any social skill, assertion training is based on behavioural therapy (practiced by some psychologists) but focuses on learning techniques rather than on understanding or explaining behaviour. It assumes that, as we can learn inappropriate behaviour, so we can learn to behave more appropriately. The focus of assertion training is, therefore, on helping individuals to develop their skills. Its benefits include:

- Improved verbal and non-verbal communication
- Reduced anxiety
- Increased control
- Improved self-awareness and self-esteem

The techniques involved are straightforward and some may come 'naturally'. However, if this is new to you, don't worry! There is more than enough information here to 'get you going'.

RIGHTS AND ASSERTIVE BEHAVIOUR

Assertive behaviour depends not only on knowing what to say or do but also on knowing how to say it. It requires that we accept that we're all entitled to certain rights; unless we know our rights, we can't decide when they are violated or when to accept or reject them. In recognising our rights we make our position clear and demonstrate our respect for ourselves or for others. Many rights have been identified; examples are shown in Table 3.1.

To be able to state needs, feelings, opinions and values: Although this is a fundamental right, it is only too easy to forget ourselves in meeting the obligations attached to our role, at work or at home. Accepting this right means simply acknowledging that we have needs and wants which are as important as those of anyone else. Indeed, at times, our needs may take priority. Recognising this is the first step on the road to change.

We also have the right to our own views, beliefs and opinions whether or not they are the same as those of others. As children we were not afraid to voice our opinions until we were told *'You mustn't*

Table 3.1   Examples of individual rights

> - To be able to state our own needs, feelings, opinions and values
> - To be treated with respect
> - To make decisions without having to justify them
> - To make mistakes
> - To refuse demands; to be able to say 'yes' or 'no' for ourselves
> - To say 'I don't understand'
> - To ask for what we want
> - Not to take responsibility for other people's problems
> - To change
> - To independence
> - To express ourselves clearly and honestly, to be assertive.

say that ...' or *'Don't be stupid ...'*. Many of us carry such negative messages into adulthood and are afraid to express our views in case we look stupid or make fools of ourselves. Perhaps we're afraid that others will think less of us, particularly when they are our superiors or hold a position of influence. It is only human to have opinions and beliefs, and it is our right to make these known.

To be treated with respect: We are all entitled to be treated with respect by others, whoever they are, but since we don't always respect ourselves how can we expect others to do so? We often fail to give ourselves credit for our ability or knowledge and it is easy to lose confidence when our arguments are challenged. It is important to remember that you *know* what you are doing rather than allowing yourself to be dominated by arguments that make you doubt your ability, knowledge or even your common sense.

To make our own decisions: As intelligent human beings we clearly have the right to make our own decisions as long as we are prepared to cope with the consequences. Of course, it is quite likely, particularly at work, that people will try to influence you, to 'persuade' you to their point of view. Their previous behaviour may also influence your decision-making, albeit subconsciously, affecting the decision you now feel able to make. Alternatively, you may worry that making a particular decision will make you unpopular. Your previous experience, and the negative feelings associated with it, make it difficult for you to behave assertively.

To make mistakes: In today's competitive environment, with its emphasis on competence and achievement, it is difficult to accept that we have the right to make mistakes. Many of us believe this is unacceptable and shows that we are 'stupid'. But we must accept that we can *do* something stupid without indicating that we *are* stupid. Accepting and *believing* this, can free us to admit our mistakes without losing our confidence or self-esteem. Thus, instead of seeing mistakes as a sign of failure deterring us from trying again, we can view them as a challenge to spur us on to 'do better'. In any case, remember that success is often built on learning from past mistakes; a positive attitude towards them, and reflecting on what you could do differently, can stimulate your development. In other words, be kind to yourself, support and encourage yourself and vow to do better next time.

> **EXERCISE:**
> Reflect on a mistake you have made. What factors contributed to it? What effects did it have - on you or on others? How could you do it differently next time? What lessons have you learned?

To be able to say 'yes' or 'no': One of the most common difficulties experienced by non-assertive people is their inability to say 'no' to even the most unreasonable request. To say no - when that is what we want to do - is a necessary skill requiring a positive attitude. It means that you can make a choice for yourself. The difficulties associated with saying yes or no are discussed further in Chapter 7.

Failure to understand: Admitting that you don't understand is not always easy. What inhibits us from speaking out? Largely it is fear of 'looking stupid'. Like admitting our mistakes, admitting a lack of understanding can be both difficult and embarrassing. We may be ashamed to acknowledge our 'ignorance'. But none of us can be expected to know everything. We should feel able to say *'I don't understand'*, *'Could you explain that again?'* or *'Could you clarify ...?'*.

Becoming assertive can help us to acknowledge confusion or lack of understanding without worrying about the consequences. Indeed, people are likely to respect our honesty.

Asking for what we want: This, in principle at least, sounds quite simple - until you ask for something that conflicts with the wishes or expectations of someone else, your manager perhaps. For example, you have booked a day off when your manager insists that you forego this to complete an important report. You feel that you have a right to your day off and he is violating your rights by being so insistent; he is behaving aggressively. When you can identify these feelings, you have accepted this right and can go on to decide how to stand up for it and how to respond.

To refuse responsibility for other people's problems: Refusing to take responsibility for the problems of others may seem selfish or unkind but it need not be that way. To decline to accept such responsibility does not mean that we should not help others to solve problems or choose to put other people first sometimes. What it does mean is that we should not allow ourselves to be 'persuaded' into taking care of others or taking over their responsibilities so that there is no time to take care of ourselves and our needs. *Choosing* to help someone else is very different but, despite our better judgement, we often give in to pressure to accommodate their needs rather than setting limits for ourselves. Accepting this right, and thinking through each situation carefully, allows us to decide where to draw the line.

To change: People often encourage us to change, particularly at work where the appraisal process, for example, often gives them the chance to point out aspects of our behaviour that they don't like or feel could be improved. However, when we start to change we may encounter resistance. For example, colleagues may regard this as threatening and be critical of the 'new you'. Such negativity may cause you to question your actions. Any change you *choose* to make must be related to your own objectives and goals - what is it that you want to achieve? Remember that success can be judged not by achievement but by the journey towards change, when you can see that you are moving in the right direction. Successful change is not judged by comparing yourself with others but with yourself - where you are compared to where you want to be. Successful change depends on knowing what you want and planning how to get there.

Independence: Accepting that you are not dependent on approval from others can be difficult. Our upbringing often meant that appropriate behaviour was rewarded while misbehaviour was punished thus creating an association between appropriate behaviour and an accepting and loving response while disapproval threatened our self-esteem. An inability to accept disapproval inhibits many of us from stating our needs, saying no or standing up for our rights. For most of us, this fear is symptomatic of our view of ourselves. The better we can develop our confidence and establish a positive dialogue with ourselves, the more effectively we can control fear and begin to accept the right to be ourselves. This takes courage but, once we realise that incurring disapproval does not bring the world to an end, it becomes increasingly easy. Our pride at handling a situation assertively will boost our morale and self-esteem and we will begin to see that we can survive without continuous approval or acceptance from others. Self-acceptance precedes true independence.

To be assertive: As you are reading this book it seems likely that you want to increase your assertiveness. Understanding the concepts of assertion, and developing your skills, will help you to relate to others in different and more personally satisfying ways. Achieving this successfully will increase the likelihood of creating the life *you* want, attaining your goals and enhancing your self-respect.

Although assertiveness is the recommended behaviour this does not mean that you *must* be assertive in all situations. It is your right to choose to be assertive or non-assertive as you feel appropriate.

RESPONSIBILITIES

Accepting the rights associated with assertion implies acceptance of the responsibilities which go hand-in-hand with them. Concentrating on your rights while ignoring your responsibilities is selfish and complete anathema to assertiveness. It also contributes to the confusion between assertiveness and aggression. One means of overcoming this is to be aware of the responsibilities associated with assertion. So, if you want to defend *your* rights assertively you must ensure that you respect the rights of others. It is only too easy to become so centred on *your* rights that you lose sight of this. For example, if you have a right to make a mistake you *must* be willing to accept that others may also do so. We must accord to others the same rights we give to ourselves.

Remember, choice is one of the central features of assertion; sticking rigidly to your rights, regardless of the situation, may be counter-productive. Choosing to forego them in particular situations is an assertive act.

PERSONAL BELIEFS: THEIR INFLUENCE ON ACCEPTANCE OF RIGHTS

We often have good intentions but cannot put them into practice; something holds us back. One of the main reasons for this is that our underlying beliefs inhibit our actions. Beliefs, defined as: *The views or opinions that we hold to be true or real about ourselves, other people or the 'world' in general; they are things about which we are absolutely certain and in which we have faith* (Back and Back, 1982), determine the rights we feel able to accept or give to others. They are formed against the background of our previous experiences and our interpretation of them. For example, as children, we may be told we're stupid when we say or do something that merits parental disapproval. If this happens regularly we may begin to believe that we *are* stupid and be reluctant to express our ideas. This may spill over into adulthood so that we behave non-assertively in various situations. We may, for example, fail to contribute to a meeting or be tentative in offering solutions to a problem. Not surprisingly, we may feel frustrated by our inability to influence the outcome thus reinforcing our belief in our stupidity and creating a vicious circle from which it is difficult to escape. Our interpretation of current situations, however, further complicates the relationship between rights and beliefs. While, in the example above, is quite clear that your ideas have been ignored the results are not always so clear and it may be possible to interpret them differently.

Your beliefs, undoubtedly, influence the way you interpret such incidents so that, if you believe you're stupid, you search for, and find, evidence to support this. This, in turn, reinforces your belief.

Thus our beliefs not only influence our behaviour but also the way we think about and interpret its effects. We seek evidence to reinforce our beliefs about ourself and rationalise anything which does not 'fit' with them.

Deciding to become assertive means that you want to do something about your beliefs, to break-away from what has become a self-fulfilling prophecy. To achieve this, you must examine your beliefs and analyse how they may be affecting you and leading you to non-assertive behaviour. Some examples are:

- Other people are more important than I am
- My opinions don't count
- People won't like me if I say what I really think
- I must get this right, I can't make a mistake.

> **EXERCISE:**
> Try to identify which of the beliefs you hold are preventing you from becoming assertive. Try to be honest but recognise that you may not be consciously aware of them and it may take time for them to become apparent. Try to think how they affect you; write notes about this and reflect on them from time to time to reinforce your desire for change.
>
> Having established the beliefs that inhibit your assertion, decide which you would like to change, but don't be too ambitious - take things slowly. A slow, gentle approach is more likely to be successful.

Modifying your beliefs

1. Remember that your beliefs are founded on your previous experiences; some may stem from childhood, others from school or work. It is likely, however, that you have modified these as you have grown and developed. Some, however, may now be outdated; knowledge you have gained since they were first formed may mean that they should now be reconsidered. For instance, to return to the example of 'stupidity' you may have formed this belief in childhood becoming unwilling to ask questions. However, during your professional career, you learned to question the material presented

and you now realise that asking questions is central to developing understanding. Even so, your underlying belief may still influence your behaviour at the weekly staff meeting. This example shows that we must examine our current beliefs in the light of our changing knowledge.

2. Studying the way other people behave, particularly someone we respect, can stimulate thoughts about our own behaviour. For instance, finding out what they think about participating in meetings and discussing this with them can provide new ideas for helping you to change your behaviour.

3. Only too often we find evidence that reinforces our beliefs about ourself. We rarely spend time or effort trying to find examples to show our strengths. So, if your beliefs are inhibiting your actions try to find examples to disprove them. For instance, if you believe that stupidity prevents you from contributing to meetings, reflect on your performance, focusing on instances where you did contribute rather than those when you did not.

4. An alternative approach is to think through the advantages of changing your beliefs and identify any effects this would have on the rights you are prepared to accept. Consider also the situations in which you might want to hold the modified belief, which assertive behaviours this might help you to adopt and the benefits this would have. Try the behaviours you have identified; it is likely that you will have positive results which will strengthen your confidence. This knowledge will help you to modify the belief concerned.

CHAPTER 3: IT AIN'T WHAT YOU DO ...

Good communication is central in determining how we get on with others. Is there a balanced exchange of views or is conversation 'one-sided', or dominated by a single individual? Does everyone feel they have had a fair hearing? Assertive communication means being able to tell others what you think, being straightforward and not 'beating around the bush' or worrying about potential disagreement. It means listening and reflecting on what you have heard. Before considering the skills required to achieve this, try this exercise:

> **EXERCISE:**
> Observe people you know who communicate assertively and try to identify what makes them effective? Make a note of your observations and compare them with the material shown below.

You will probably find that effective communicators take care to attract and retain the listener's attention They will speak clearly and loudly enough to ensure that they're heard, articulating clearly and stressing important words or phrases. Their actions and words will be congruent and, by taking views in turn, they will that ensure everyone is heard. This promotes balanced conversations allowing an exchange of views and feelings which is usually satisfactory to all involved (Sharpe, 1989).

COMMUNICATION SKILLS

Effective communication comes naturally to some while others find this a difficult skill to acquire. However communication, like assertion, can be learned. The following are central to assertive communication:

- Effective (active) listening
- Seeking clarification and avoiding assumptions
- Appropriate use of open and closed questions
- Use of 'I' statements
- Using a 'common language'
- Appropriate body language (Chapter 4).

Effective listening: It is important to realise that listening differs from hearing, a passive activity describing the sense through which sound is perceived. In contrast, listening is an active process which requires concentration, comprehension and evaluation. It means attending not only to what people are saying but also to *how* they are saying it. The tone of voice and the emphasis placed on particular words will show what is important. Good listeners really try to understand what is being said and show that the 'message' has been received and understood. People undoubtedly know when someone is really listening and when they are not. You can show this both verbally and non-verbally by, for example, looking at others while they are talking and nodding to indicate interest. Good listeners demonstrate their willingness to listen by leaning slightly forward and facing the other person.

You may, at times, notice that there are incongruities between *what* someone is saying and *how* they are saying it although, when busy or under pressure, this is easy to overlook thus giving a negative impression and discouraging further communication. Reflecting what is being said, rephrasing it slightly, may encourage elaboration. For example:

    '... and they made me feel very welcome.'
    'So you feel that the company is interested in its new employees?
or: *'... and this made me feel very uncomfortable.'*
    'So you're finding it difficult to cope with the change?'

Reflection shows that you're listening and trying to understand without being judgmental or analytical. It also helps to ensure true understanding rather than assumption. However, if overused, it may sound strange and is best used with acknowledgement responses that indicate interest but don't disrupt the speaker's flow. Use reflection when you want to clarify meaning or when someone is talking about personal issues or their feelings or emotions.

Active listening has several advantages. It reduces the likelihood of misunderstanding and demonstrates empathy rather than sympathy or criticism, showing your acceptance of the speaker. It may also help to defuse emotion. Lastly, concentrating on listening will prevent you from 'talking over' others encouraging them to explore problems for themselves.

> **EXERCISE: Improving your listening skills**
> Study the way you behave when listening. Ask yourself if:
> - You tend to finish off people's sentences or do you allow them to finish what they are saying?
> - You assume that you know what people are going to say and 'talk over' them while they are still talking?
> - You maintain eye contact while you're talking?
> - You use reflection or seek clarification when you don't understand?
> - You 'listen' to what you're thinking or 'filter' what is being said so that you hear only what you want to hear?

Your answers will help you to identify what you need to do in order to improve your listening skills.

Seeking clarification: Although reflection can be helpful this is not always the best way of gaining understanding. Clarification is particularly useful here. For example, when you are unclear about the key point in a discussion or the purpose of a meeting you are probably not alone. Thus, by seeking clarification, you will help both yourself and others who are also confused or unclear. This can save time and misunderstanding. For example: *'So what you are saying is ...?'*, *'Do you mean that we should ...?'* or *'Am I right in thinking ...?'*.

Avoiding assumptions: It is easy to make assumptions about what people are saying when you are busy or under pressure. 'Jumping to conclusions' is a common source of misunderstanding. Take care to ensure that you really understand what has been said.

Open and closed questions: Good communication depends on mutual understanding and careful listening. Appropriate questions can aid clarification and overcome assumptions. As long as they are open, inviting a response, questions can also help to develop communication. Open questions cannot be answered with a straight 'yes' or 'no' but require an answer in the respondent's own words enabling you to elicit feelings and attitudes as well as facts. They can help to expand on issues, encourage the sharing of information, and help a conversation to expand rather than closing it off.

Open questions are those beginning with 'what', 'how', 'why', 'when' and 'which'. Thus, for example, a closed question, such as *'Do you like working at Smiths?'* encourages a one word answer while the open-ended *'What do you like most about working at Smiths?'* requires greater expansion. Encouraging others to expand on their thoughts or feelings is assertive and shows interest in them as individuals.

Although useful in obtaining specific information, closed questions, tend to direct respondents towards the required answer (i.e. directive or leading questions). For example: *'Don't you think its disgraceful that we can't get coffee until 11 o'clock?'* clearly indicates the desired answer. The speaker wants you to agree with him! Closed questions are useful when trying to summarise or clarify material or to force an admission (as in a trial). They can also help when you want to control those who will not stop talking and you want to bring the conversation to an end!

EXERCISE:
Think about the way you participate in conversations. What type of questions do you use? When do you use them? Is this appropriate? Do you use open questions as a way of finding out how others are feeling and what they are thinking about the issues under discussion?

Examining your use of open and closed questions will help you to identify areas where change may be required.

Use of 'I' statements: Being assertive means taking responsibility for your actions. One of the easiest ways to demonstrate this is to use 'I' statements which allow you to present your view clearly and unambiguously. When you lack confidence you are much less likely to be so direct. 'I' statements help to distinguish opinion from fact and emphasise that you are presenting **your** views based on **your** knowledge or experience. For example, when making a suggestion it is more effective to say, *'I think ...'* or *'I would like to suggest ...'* rather than *'Don't you think ...?'*.

'I' statements are also useful when developing new relationships, helping you to disclose information about yourself and open up a conversation, identify common ground and help others to relax.

However, don't overdo it as it may be interpreted as an attempt to take over or monopolise the conversation! Ideally, disclosure should be matched with each person 'taking turns'. This helps you to gain a close relationship by allowing you to share your feelings, attitudes and beliefs.

Using self-disclosure effectively requires practice, particularly at work. It is easy to cause discomfort or embarrassment or to dominate the conversation so that others feel unable to 'escape'. This reduces the likelihood of developing a reciprocal relationship. Thus the *appropriateness* of your disclosure is extremely important. While increasing the intimacy of disclosure may be appropriate to personal friendships this may not be true in developing working relationships.

EXERCISE:
Try developing a conversation by using self-disclosure and 'I' statements that make it quite clear that you are talking about yourself and not making generalisations. Talking about yourself like this is likely to lead others to believe that you are open and disclosing and mean that you are someone they might like to know better.

Using a common language: If you have ever met with a group of people with shared expertise (such as doctors, nurses or lawyers) you may know how it feels to be excluded from the conversation by jargon that they understand but which, of necessity, excludes those who are not 'in the know'. They are comfortable talking together, using a form of verbal 'shorthand' which ensures that they are all on the same 'wavelength'. It is less helpful when talking to a newcomer or an outsider who may feel that they are 'stupid' or 'invisible'.

We use words as symbols to express our thoughts, ideas, beliefs and feelings. These combine with the other symbolic and non-verbal means of communication to transmit our 'message'. Communication has only been effective when that 'message' has been received and understood. This is much easier when those involved are on the same wavelength thus, two nurses, or two mechanics, are likely to use the same words with the same meanings. Think about how you might feel when trying to elicit information from either of these groups; you may need to seek clarification several times before you fully understand. Try not to exclude people from your conversations.

The second important element of effective communication is establishing some common ground. In the example, above the nurses or mechanics share experiences; in other situations, this may, however, not be so easy. A nurse and a mechanic in conversation may have greater difficulty in establishing a rapport.

Our different backgrounds and experiences mean that we inevitably have different beliefs and attitudes so that we don't necessarily see eye-to-eye with everyone but, if we are to communicate effectively, we need to find something in common. This is why we use 'social chit-chat' to 'break the ice'. We talk, for example, about the weather or the journey to work. Similarly, an interview often starts with a simple question, the equivalent of social conversation, to relax the candidate.

COMMUNICATION IN THE WORKPLACE

Good communication is essential at all levels of the working environment and is central to good management. Since management is often defined as 'getting things done through other people' the importance of effective communication cannot be overemphasised. Such communication requires two-way interaction with senior managers, colleagues and subordinates and necessitates not only good verbal skills but also effective listening to ensure understanding of other people's perspective. There are many examples of managers who have heard what people have said but have failed to fully understand it, leading to misunderstanding and/or disagreement. It is highly likely that you have experience of this since the most common criticism of managers is that they do not listen.

This often arises because managers are primarily interested in the long- or medium-term, in strategies, plans and objectives while employees are more interested in practicalities such as working arrangements, shortage of staff, rewards and day-to-day activity. Effective communication is of prime importance in the workplace and is critical in ensuring that everyone is working towards a common goal.

Thus, managers who want to be recognised as good communicators must demonstrate both the ability to listen and good conversational skills that enable relationships to be developed. A manager wanting to deal with his or her staff, colleagues and clients successfully must be able to open the conversation by establishing common ground and use open questions to obtain information. Judicious use of self-disclosure can also be useful helping to build trust.

CHAPTER 4: ... IT'S THE WAY THAT YOU DO IT

It is often said that you have only to enter a room for someone to form an opinion of you and how you feel. The 'picture' you present may say more about you than any words you use. This is created by your posture, gestures, facial expression and other non-verbal signs, in other words, by your body language. Indeed, it is generally agreed that between 60% and 80% of all communication is conveyed through non-verbal means. Pease (1981), an expert in body language, reports that verbal 'channels' are used primarily for transferring information while non-verbal signs convey interpersonal attitudes.

Thus, effective communication requires some understanding of body language since, without this, we can neither examine our own behaviours nor pick up others' non-verbal cues. It is important to study our own behaviour if we are to understand why our communication is not always as effective as we would like it to be. Our body language may distort the message we are trying to convey.

BODY LANGUAGE

Remember the success of the 'silent' movies which depended solely on the skill and ability of their stars to convey their meaning using only gestures, facial expressions and other body signals? What better example to show how communicative body language can be? Few people recognise the way that their posture, movements and gestures can affect the interpretation of what they are saying. Indeed, body language may tell one story while their words tell another. This lack of congruity may be important since Pease (1981) shows that non-verbal cues carry about five times more impact than words and, where there is incongruity between the two, people rely on the non-verbal rather than the verbal message.

Thus attempts to be assertive may be unsuccessful not because you have used the wrong words but because your body reveals uncertainty or self-doubt. In other words, your body has 'joined in' the conversation to contradict what you are saying and confuse the listener. Thus, when developing assertiveness, it is worth devoting some time to trying to understand the influence of body language in supporting your hard won skills.

First impressions

The significance of body language during the first five minutes of any interaction cannot be overemphasised. Even while we are making small talk we are forming a lasting impression that can radically affect the outcome.

Physical appearance provides information about age, sex and 'attractiveness'. It may also suggest status which may be important as most people will, for example, be more polite if they think someone holds a position superior to their own. Similarly, we all enjoy looking at someone who is physically attractive, whether they are male or female. Posture, gestures and facial expressions are also noted.

For example, facial expressions are dynamic and constantly changing and, when we look at someone, we can readily tell whether they're interested or bored, cheerful or unhappy. In general, a mobile and expressive face is believed to belong to a more interesting and warm personality than one that is inscrutable and static. The face can also reveal emotions. For example, fear, anxiety and sadness are seen in the eyes while shock or surprise are revealed by raised eyebrows and wide-open eyes, accompanied by a gasp or an open mouth.

Of course, while we are looking, we are also listening and gathering additional information from the voice. Although we may pay little attention to the content of 'small talk' we do pay attention to its sound. We can learn a great deal from the tone, volume and pitch of the voice. For example, booming volume suggests dominance or aggression while quiet voices may suggest submission or passivity; thin or weak voices do not inspire confidence. Evenly paced speech, with subtle alterations in pitch and volume to emphasise important points, inspires greatest confidence and trust.

Eye contact is also important and 'speaks' volumes about individuals. Indeed, research has shown that eye contact can be used to regulate conversations. When these are friendly, people will look at one another frequently but only for short periods of time. Longer eye contact is used when one person wants to dominate, or even threaten, another while minimal eye contact creates a negative impression suggesting submission or dishonesty. Care is needed, however, since many painfully shy people have found themselves labelled as 'shifty' due to their inability to look others in the eye!

This discussion shows that a significant amount of information is 'transmitted' not by anything that is said but through non-verbal means. Although a fuller 'picture' is developed as the interaction proceeds this is 'filed away' and may be difficult to change.

What does your body language say about you?

By now you can see that your body communicates as clearly as your words and, because it so closely reflects what and how we feel, it is important that we act assertively in order to feel assertive.

Facial expression: The look on your face undoubtedly contributes strongly to the overall impression that you create. If you are frowning or your eyes are downcast you will appear to be worried or on the defensive. Alternatively, if your jaw is clenched or your chin is jutting out you may be feeling tense or aggressive.

To improve the effectiveness of your communication it is helpful to keep your head upright, nodding and smiling where appropriate. This indicates that you are actively involved in the interaction and may encourage others to 'open up' and be more direct and honest; smiling can also encourage intimacy. Moving from a relaxed posture and leaning forward for a few seconds can emphasise points that are particularly important or which you feel strongly about. Combining these approaches with effective listening (page 18) provides a sound basis for developing assertive communication.

Take care however not to smile inappropriately. If you are trying to indicate that you're hurt or angry, or attempting to end a conversation, you will not be taken seriously if you have a broad smile on your face. You will confuse others when your message is not congruent with your body language.

Eye contact: The eyes clearly indicate whether someone is interested in what you're saying, intimidated or simply not listening. Seeing 'eye-to-eye' often indicates the beginning of real communication. This suggests that the amount of eye contact is critically important when developing relationships. Indeed, although we may feel quite comfortable when talking to some people, others make us feel ill-at-ease. This is primarily due to the length of time that they look at us during our conversation. Have you ever tried to talk to someone wearing sunglasses, when you can't see whether they're looking at you or how they are reacting to what you're saying? Pease (1981) suggests that, when someone is being dishonest or withholding information, their eyes meet yours infrequently, probably for less than 30% of the time. When their gaze meets yours for longer (about 65%) it may mean one of two things. If they find what you are saying very interesting their pupils will be dilated. Alternatively, they may be hostile towards you or to what you are saying when the pupils will be constricted. He or she is issuing a non-verbal challenge.

To build a good rapport with another person your eyes should meet his for 60-70% of the time. Remember that it is difficult to talk to someone who looks at you directly without shifting their gaze. This can be very disconcerting and uncomfortable for the recipient. To demonstrate confidence do not be afraid to look directly at the other person maintaining firm but friendly eye contact while making an assertive request or statement. The ability to do this can greatly reinforce the message you are trying to convey.

> **EXERCISE:**
> Practise making eye contact with someone as you are talking. Are you aware of any differences in the quality of your communication? Are you conveying or receiving greater interest in what you are saying? Compare this with conversations in which eye contact is minimal.

When involved in formal or work-based discussions, Pease (1981) suggests we can maintain control of the interaction by appropriate use of eye contact. He suggests that we should imagine a triangle on the other person's forehead in which his eyes form the base and the apex is in the middle of his forehead. Directing your gaze at this area shows that you mean business. As long as your gaze does not fall below the level of the other's eyes you will maintain control.

Gestures: Accentuating your words with appropriate gestures can add strength to any communication, allowing you to demonstrate emphasis, openness and warmth. Some gestures, such as fiddling with your hair or clasping and unclasping your hands, are easily recognised signs of anxiety. Drumming your fingers on the table or shuffling/tapping your feet suggests impatience or embarrassment. Although pointing at others can be irritating the fingers can be used for emphasis by, for example, using them to 'count off' points.

In assertive communication your body and especially your arms, should suggest openness. You should avoid creating any barriers (e.g. arms folded across your chest) between you and the others involved; these can make you look defensive or unapproachable.

> **EXERCISE:**
> Study the gestures you use and practise, in role play, avoiding those which create the impression of non-assertion. Identify those gestures you use which may be considered aggressive or passive and plan a strategy to help you to change the way you behave when you would like to demonstrate your assertion.

Voice: Your voice is probably one of the most important tools you can use in developing assertiveness. People who speak very loudly or barely above a whisper can be irritating although, clearly, if you want to make a point you may need to increase the volume of your voice to project your words. This does not, however, mean raising its pitch. Indeed, you can often produce a dramatic effect by keeping your voice lower than those around you, particularly in difficult situations when others may be concerned that they will miss something important and drop the volume of their speech in order to hear you more clearly. Practise using both the higher and lower registers of your voice to find that which is most appropriate for use in different situations. Remember that the difference between assertive and non-assertive communication often lies in subtle differences in the pitch and tone of voice used. A lower pitched voice is most commonly associated with assertion.

Clearly, body language has an important role in all aspects of communication. It can enhance of detract from your message. The interested reader is advised to read the work of Alan Pease (1981) for further information.

CHAPTER 5: CONFLICT AND DISAGREEMENT

Dealing with criticism is difficult, whether we are on the giving or receiving end. It can be particularly difficult at work when criticism is often interpreted as comment on the person rather than their work. Thus, without careful handling, criticism may damage working relationships. This need not occur. Guidance for handling both the giving and receiving of criticism assertively is given here.

GIVING CRITICISM

Talking about unsatisfactory aspects of performance is a difficult, but necessary, task that many of us fear. Before we tackle it, we must be clear about our motives. Do we want to give straightforward and honest criticism designed to help individuals to improve or do we simply want to put them down? The former may help us both; the latter is destructive, has little effect on performance and damages relationships. We must also remember that criticism is a means to an end and not an end in itself.

One of the best ways to approach this is to consider how *we* handle criticism distinguishing that which is helpful and constructive from that which is negative and destructive. This can help us to decide how best to deliver criticism. Many of us put off the 'evil moment' or raise our criticism tentatively hoping that the situation will improve. Alternatively, we allow negative feelings to build working ourselves into an angry state so that, when we raise the issue, we do so aggressively. Again the required improvement in performance does not occur and we become increasingly angry.

Assertive people regard criticism positively as providing them with the opportunity to grow and develop. They see the emphasis as lying in future changes in their performance rather than as a negative emphasis on the past. Thus an assertive critic will approach criticism constructively. They will:

- Be impersonal, labelling the behaviour not the person
- Acknowledge the positive, balancing criticism with appreciation
- Be specific and avoid generalisations
- Be constructive, offering suggestions for improvement and

helping to identify the cause of difficulties
- Keep to the point avoiding the temptation to bring in all their other complaints and confuse the issue
- Keep calm.

> **Exercise:**
> With a partner, practise giving criticism to each other. Keep this light-hearted and focus, perhaps, on each other's clothes or cooking skills. Take turns in doing this, providing feedback to the other. Was their criticism helpful and constructive? Was it impersonal? Did they offer suggestions for improvement?

Since, when giving criticism, you are usually taking the initiative you can select an appropriate time to do this. This will give you time to prepare during which you can clarify your purpose and motives, specify the criticism and identify some positive aspects of the other's performance. One way of achieving this is to use the 4:1 principle in providing criticism (i.e. four positive comments to each critical one).

Ask yourself what you wish to change about the other's performance. Are they, perhaps, often late in submitting work, taking too long over meal breaks or producing substandard work? Clear, factual statements, specifying your criticism, will help to ensure that it is not seen as an attack on the person or their integrity. For example:

- State how the criticism has arisen. *'I've had several complaints about the late submission of your work.'*
- Point out its effects on you or your department. *'I've had some difficulty in justifying ...'*
- Show how this affects the individual. *'I think this may affect the work you're allocated in the future.'*

These approaches will, undoubtedly, improve your ability to deliver criticism when it is needed.

RECEIVING CRITICISM

It is natural to be defensive when criticised. We often remember being hurt by criticism as children and so tend to view it negatively. But, remember that assertive people see criticism positively but take care to distinguish between that which is helpful and that which says more about the other person than it does about them.

In practice, few of us are invulnerable to criticism; we often find it distressing and difficult to accept. Most of us would admit to responding in various ways. For example, we may take all possible steps to avoid being in a position where we can be criticised or find ourselves using passive or ingratiating behaviours. When criticised we may react aggressively using our 'natural defences' to retaliate immediately. This often leads to a 'slanging match' getting us nowhere, doing little to resolve our difficulties and damaging our relationships. Alternatively, we may take even unfair or unjustified criticism to heart, particularly if our confidence is low when it is easy to overreact, absorbing and acting on criticism even when disagreeing with our critic. Lastly we may allow our anger and resentment to build until they 'erupt' at some inappropriate time.

These are not assertive reactions. Assertive people are not afraid of criticism; they know how to deal with it. They recognise that criticism may be useful or useless, valid or invalid; it may be reasonable or unreasonable. We must decide which of these describes a particular piece of criticism and how we want to react to it. It is easy to accept criticism simply because 'someone says so', whether or not it is fair or valid. To deal with this ask yourself:

- Is this fact or opinion?
- Should it be acknowledged or rejected?
- Is it appropriate or inappropriate?
- Is this criticism a useful source of feedback?

Facts may be difficult to refute and, if you have made mistakes, you may learn how to avoid these in the future. Remember that you have a right to make mistakes and don't let them destroy you but ensure that you learn from them. Opinions are less important; others' opinions are largely their concern and we can decide whether we want to take them into account. Facts should be acknowledged and can then be accepted or rejected as appropriate.

Three techniques can be used to help us to deal with criticism assertively: fogging, negative enquiry and negative assertion.

Fogging is useful in dealing with criticism that is designed to 'put you down', make you feel bad about yourself or manipulate you into doing something that you don't want to do. Although there may be an element of truth in such criticism this is often exaggerated. For example, *'You're late! You're always late. You're so selfish. You don't care about anyone else ...'.*

If you *are* late the criticism is justified. The elaboration, however, is designed to trigger guilt. Fogging can help you to deal with this by acknowledging the truth while preventing manipulation or damage to your self-esteem. So, in the example above, you would say something like: *'Yes, I am late this morning, perhaps I should try to leave home earlier.'* This deflects your critic; you have refused to reward his put down behaviour and have not responded as he has anticipated so that he is less likely to try again.

Negative enquiry actively requires you to seek constructive criticism. This can be difficult, but will help you to develop a better understanding of your behaviour. It implies that you are willing to compromise or change. It also provides a way of establishing whether your critic is genuinely concerned or simply wanting to put you down. Once you have established his true intention you can decide how best to deal with it. An example would be:

Critic: *'I think you'll find that report difficult because your writing isn't up to standard'*

An assertive response, using negative enquiry, would be:

'In what ways is my writing not up to standard?'

The response will quickly illustrate the critic's intention. A genuine concern will be shown by a comment such as:

'I've noticed that it takes you a long time to get started and that you seem to have difficulties in structuring your work.'

He may then offer to help or add a compliment designed to encourage you; *'But, I noticed that the work you did on Smith's account was well done and took you less time.'*

However, using negative enquiry may extract a less helpful response, especially if the criticism was designed to put you down. The approach may simply continue and lack specificity. *'Well, I don't know. You wouldn't really want to know what I think, you ought to get help from someone who knows what they're doing.'* You can do little about this other than acknowledge its negativity.

Negative assertion: This involves you in calmly agreeing with any criticism provided, of course, that you believe it is valid and justified. For example:

Critic: *'Your office is a tip. You're hopelessly disorganised.'*
You: *'Yes, it's true, I'm not very organised.'*

Here you acknowledge the criticism and demonstrate your acceptance of it. This can be difficult and often seems as if you're putting yourself down. However, if you're prepared to admit your faults, people will be less likely to criticise you or put you down.

The ability to use negative assertion depends on a high degree of self-awareness and willingness to recognise your faults which, in turn, depends on self-confidence. Although few of us are perfect acknowledging our faults can help us to do something about them.

ANGER

It is not unusual to feel angry, irritated or frustrated or to come across these feelings in others. They are, simply, facts of life. It is important to explore their effects since knowing more about them can help us to take active steps to deal with them more effectively.

Since anger is often an overwhelming emotion, and can be very destructive, it is difficult to deal with. This may, in part, reflect our upbringing that often discourages us from expressing such emotions so that we 'bottle them up' and deny them. This may seem simpler than trying to work out what we feel or what to do about it. Perhaps we feel helpless believing that it is useless to try to solve the problem; we often lose heart, sinking into despair, resignation and acceptance. In the long-term this is to our disadvantage as suppressing such feelings may allow them to build until they 'erupt' at some later, often inappropriate, time. They may also add to our stress. Yet many of us are used to receiving messages that discourage us from expressing anger (e.g. count to ten before you respond). The net effect is that some people are so controlled that they do not openly express their anger.

> **EXERCISE:**
> Try to identify particular times or specific situations when you get angry. Do they share common characteristics? How does anger make you feel? Thinking through anger in this way will help to identify those things likely to provoke it and to think about the effects it has on you. Armed with this information you may be able to find ways of managing such situations more effectively or, perhaps, avoiding them altogether.

It is not unusual to feel angry sometimes. What varies is the way we deal with it (Table 5.1). For most of us, anger is an aggressive response to a situation in which we feel the need to 'punish' others. Because we're sure we're right anger from others may make us doubt the validity of our views, damaging our self-esteem. In effect, our anger is an attempt to 'persuade' others that we're right thus boosting our self-esteem. When this fails, as aggression often does, we're left with feelings of discomfort and even guilt and, to make matters worse, we have not solved the problem. Anger can, therefore, have adverse effects on those involved potentiating power conflicts in which all parties retain their beliefs in their position. This may exacerbate the situation leading one or more participants 'to go over the top'; emotions run high clouding the issue with neither party listening to the other.

Conversely, anger can help to relieve stress and to 'clear the air'. The 'trick' is to use it constructively so that it enhances openness and helps to build trust. However, anger can motivate us to change our lives or the lives of those around us. For example, if some people didn't feel angry about injustice, many social problems would not be resolved. Anger about poverty or homelessness has led many to try to improve the plight of the disadvantaged and, without the anger felt by the suffragettes, women would still be disenfranchised. So, when channelled constructively, anger can help us to achieve great things! It spurs us on enhancing our wish to overcome problems. However, if you have ever felt guilty about being angry, or about expressing it, perhaps fearing you have appeared harsh, uncaring or threatening, you may want to change the way you do this so that you don't hurt either yourself or others in the process.

Table 5.1   Responses to anger

Some situations likely to provoke anger	Some feelings which may accompany anger
Feeling threatened, frightened or inadequate	Self-righteousness
	Low self-esteem
Failure to get 'our own way'	Indignation
Violation of our rights	Excitement
Feeling the need to 'defend' ourselves	Powerlessness
	Feeling powerful
Feeling hurt	Loss of control
Being wronged	Tension in the neck, shoulders or jaw
Injustice	
Stupidity	Flushing
Incompetence in others	Racing pulse
Being ignored or taken for granted	Sweating
	Breathlessness

All too often anger is expressed indirectly. Dickson (1982) identifies four strategies which may be adopted as ways of doing this. They are, the Disruptor, the Spoiler, the Deflator and the Stoker.

The Disruptor, a 'mischief-maker', makes apparently innocent remarks or asks naive questions sowing the seeds of doubt or discontent. This goes almost unnoticed but, by initiating doubt, increases the likelihood of conflict, quarrels and disagreement.

The Spoiler always manages to ask for something at precisely the wrong moment! You have just reached the end of a long, difficult meeting when a pressing issue is raised and demands attention. Plans will be subtly sabotaged or the Spoiler will butt in with irrelevant comments that demonstrate failure to listen. His or her frustration and tension are such that he finds ways of spoiling things for others.

The Deflator: At the very point of success the Deflator will try to belittle it. Your success acts as a spur to such people who, just as you are feeling proud of your achievement, will say something like: *'Well, I don't know what you're going on about, it wasn't that difficult.'*

Resentment is expressed indirectly; in all probability, the Deflator is jealous of your success.

The Stoker: Just as the stoker on a train keeps the fires alight so the Stoker will complain endlessly and dredge up old grievances. Although they may complain of over-work they will consistently refuse all offers of help. They will be a 'martyr' stoking anger and frustration until you 'erupt' with fury. This strategy is designed to promote anger in others; as long as they keep 'stoking' someone else will get angry for them.

> **EXERCISE:**
> A. Refer back to the exercise on page 35 and consider whether you can recognise any of these characteristics in yourself. This will help you to understand your behaviour and take steps to overcome any difficulties.
> B. Consider whether any of these people exist in your working environment. Again, recognising these characteristics in others will make it easier to understand what is going on and find ways of managing the situation.

It is possible, nay desirable, to express anger without hurting others. Open, honest and spontaneous expression can help to prevent destructive effects. Even if assertive expression does not gain you what you want, it will help to reduce the anger you might direct at yourself if you do nothing thus helping to reduce stress.

In expressing anger you must accept responsibility for your feelings. *You* are angry about what has happened. Develop and practise using assertive methods for expressing your anger. If possible:

- Take a few moments to consider if the situation is worth your time and energy as well as the possible consequences of expressing your anger
- Be spontaneous and direct about what you feel
- Avoid sarcasm and innuendo, name-calling, put-downs and physical attack
- Use 'I' language to show that you're taking responsibility for your feelings. Statements like: *'I'm very angry ...'* or *'I*

strongly disagree ...' are useful
- Seek solutions rather than allocating blame or looking for 'victory'.

Dealing with anger in others

Learning to handle anger that is directed towards us is another essential skill. The following may help to defuse the situation.

- Allow the angry person to express strong feelings
- Acknowledge that you have heard him or her. Say things like: *'I know you are angry about ...'* or *'It's obvious that you're very upset about ...'*. This will often be enough to calm the other person enabling discussion to take place. If this is not effective, take a deep breath and try to stay calm
- Use assertive statements such as: *'I would really like to talk to you about this. As soon as you're calm I'll be happy to talk to you'*. Use this as a 'broken record' (page 48) until the person calms down
- Once they are calm ensure that you listen to what they have to say
- If the situation remains emotionally charged - leave. Say that you are leaving but offer to talk about the situation later. Alternatively, just leave; don't feel that you must stick it out; this will achieve little and is unlikely to resolve the situation.

Before you try this in 'real life', role play it with a friend until you feel confident about what you're doing. Ask for supportive feedback and suggestions for improvement.

MANAGING DISAGREEMENT

Your background and experience inevitably differ from other people; this, undoubtedly, influences the way you see events. Even in the same situation you may find that your views differ. This is not surprising but, too often, leads to conflict. This is unfortunate as effective problem-solving and decision-making rely on hearing different views and interpretations; agreement and disagreement are central to these processes. Yet it is not uncommon for such situations to turn into a 'battle of wits' where aggression and 'point scoring' are rife. The effects, almost inevitably, are destructive; the issue(s) under discussion are forgotten as emotion takes over and new ideas, or valid but alternative views, are not heard. This, in turn, means that decisions made, or conclusions reached, are often not as effective as they could have been had emotions not been allowed to intervene.

Non-assertive behaviour often exaggerates conflict in situations where there is disagreement. The aggressor dismisses other people's views; they also tend to state opinions as facts and to 'dig themselves in' so that they can no longer see any alternative views. Domination by aggression often exacerbates passivity inhibiting others from contributing. Passive individuals will, in any case, think their opinions are less important. They may 'retreat' while becoming increasingly frustrated by the course of the discussion. Any challenge or disagreement will be expressed tentatively or apologetically even when their contribution is valid or valuable. It is likely that conclusions will be reached to which not all participants are truly committed.

Assertion can overcome many of these difficulties since it permits open and honest expression of both agreement and disagreement allowing you to make your position absolutely clear. And, in so doing, you do not put either yourself or others down. It recognises that there may be different, and perhaps conflicting, views and takes account of the fact that, although opinions may differ, they are not necessarily right or wrong, just different.

Constructive disagreement

Make your disagreement quite clear using 'I' statements which distinguish your views from others and demonstrate your ownership of them. This allows you to show that your experience, or underlying beliefs, differ from those of others. Examples include: *'As I see it ...', 'I don't go along with ...', In my experience ...', 'I believe ...'.*

Don't forget that you have a right to change your mind if you are swayed by the force of an argument. Be honest and acknowledge it clearly using phrases such as: *'John's argument convinces me that ...', 'In the light of ...'* or *'I now think ...'.* If, on the other hand, you are not convinced by what you hear, make this equally clear giving reasons for your disagreement. *'I don't agree with that decision because ...'.* But, at times, you may find that you agree with parts of an argument while disagreeing with others. Again there are constructive and assertive ways of making this known by focusing on those parts with which you agree and clarifying those with which you disagree. *'I agree that there is a problem with x but I don't agree that it affects all departments in the same way'*. You may wish to clarify such statements by saying *why* you feel this way.

It is also useful to acknowledge that you recognise other peoples' views even though you disagree with their perspective. This can be achieved with statements like: *'I realise that the effects on your Department are ... but, in my Department, ...'*.

The effect of using assertive techniques in managing disagreement should now be clear. They should ensure that information, different views and new ideas do not become lost in a sea of emotion, issues are not avoided and constructive discussion follows.

In summary then, anger and conflict are most easily resolved when those involved:

- Act honestly and directly towards each other
- Accept responsibility for their feelings
- Face the problem openly rather than hiding from it
- Remain impersonal and to stick to pertinent issues
- Seek solutions rather than allocating blame
- Emphasise points of agreement thus providing a foundation against which to discuss areas of disagreement
- Negotiate towards a mutually agreed compromise or simply 'agree to disagree'.

Recognition that anger is inevitable from time to time, and allowing its expression in a non-destructive way, will create conditions in which it should be possible to work towards effective resolution of problems and avoidance of conflict.

CHAPTER 6: FEEDBACK AND PRAISE

We all need feedback from those around us; we also need to know what effects we have on others. The last chapter considered giving and receiving criticism; here we focus on compliments and praise. Both are rare in most working environments, perhaps because they can be difficult both to give and to receive.

GIVING PRAISE

We often expect high standards from others and so tend to take their work and achievements for granted. Not surprising then that we hear comments like, *'I only hear from the boss when something is wrong. He never says anything good.'* Indeed, in some environments, praise is so rare that recipients are suspicious when it is offered.

Failure to give praise, however, means that people are left wondering whether their work is of an appropriate standard. Greater use of praise would, undoubtedly, change the atmosphere of many workplaces. Further, there may well be times when you want to acknowledge the quality of work achieved or compliment someone on a good idea.

There are many reasons why people are reluctant to use praise. Many of these are based on their underlying beliefs such as:

- If I praise them they'll think they needn't work so hard
- They're only doing their job
- They'll be suspicious if I offer praise
- People will only improve if you point out their mistakes.

Other reasons for reluctance to offer praise include a fear that it may be embarrassing or that it may not be well received. Some are concerned that *'I won't be able to find the right words'*. Because our experience is that it is more common to be criticised when things are going badly, we rarely tell people when they do well. However, failure to use praise can have negative effects. For example, we may be seen as critical or harsh because our criticism is never balanced by praise. Working relationships may, therefore, be less productive.

The discomfort associated with giving praise means that, if it is done at all, it is often done non-assertively. Unfortunately praise is often used manipulatively, using sarcasm or insincere compliments, to help us to get our own way. Praise can be given aggressively, passively or assertively.

The aggressive approach may lead to praise being given grudgingly and often unwillingly. For example:

- Saying something positive about what others have done while also complaining that they haven't done it before. *'Jo, that was much better, why didn't you do it like that before?'*
- Taking something for granted and assuming that it will be done well. *'Don't get big-headed it's only what we expect.'*
- Wording praise clumsily so that the implication is not clear. For example: *'That was an interesting report Jane, did Mary help you with it?'* thus implying that Jane could not have done it on her own
- Taking away a compliment by adding criticism straight away. *'That was a nice presentation but ...'*
- Overdoing praise; this may seem patronising or insincere.

The passive approach often involves being over-apologetic or hesitant as in: *'I hope you don't mind my saying so but I thought your work was excellent'* or adding: *'I wish I could do something as good as that'* thus putting yourself down. Alternatively, you may hold back from giving compliments for fear of having them rejected.

The assertive approach. Since people learn as much from their successes as their mistakes, acknowledging their performance is an important part of their continuing development. Giving praise assertively makes it quite clear to those concerned that you are talking to them and showing that their work has met your expectations. Expressing praise assertively clearly indicates that the required standard has been achieved, provided that your compliments or praise are sincere; don't use false flattery to try to make people feel good. Tips for giving praise follow:

- Specify exactly what it is that someone has said or done (or how they have done it) that you like. For example: *'I liked your report. I thought it was a good idea to highlight ...'*
- Keep praise brief and clear. Don't 'pad it out' with

- unnecessary superlatives
- Use 'I' statements
- Thank them for their contribution if appropriate
- Use the person's name to make it clear that you are referring to them. *'James, I liked the way ...'*
- Maintain eye contact.

This approach both praises the individual and gives him or her information about the standard required and the way you would like him or her to perform in future. It also increases the likelihood that your praise is seen as sincere rather than as mindless flattery.

RECEIVING PRAISE

Receiving praise can often be equally difficult. All too often the receiver feels embarrassed or foolish, thus responding defensively. They dismiss what others say in a variety of ways. They may, for example, unintentionally ridicule the other person as their defensive reactions make his efforts seem inappropriate. Instead of accepting praise graciously many of us respond non-assertively perhaps shrugging it off or feeling that we must respond in kind. Alternatively we think it immodest to accept praise and try to put the credit elsewhere or deny our achievements or expertise.

We may be aggressive indicating that it was no more than we expected or putting ourself down. *'Well I don't know, I thought that work was second-rate myself'*. This also challenges the other's judgement making them feel unsure about what you think they have said and making it unlikely that they will wish to repeat the performance, however good your future work may be.

Alternatively, some of us believe that accepting praise means that we must be grateful for it or that it creates an obligation to the person delivering it. Have you ever wondered what 'someone is after' when you have been given a compliment? Why should this be? If we have done something well why should we not be complimented for it? Although compliments and praise may be used manipulatively we are in danger of rejecting all praise indiscriminately whether or not it is justified. This is to our disadvantage.

The assertive response. The first step in receiving praise assertively is to ensure that you fully understand the nature of the praise you have been offered. If you are not sure, ask the other person to clarify what they have said (see positive enquiry below). This will help you to identify those times when praise is being used mechanically or manipulatively. Once you are sure that praise is sincere, practise a straightforward and simple acknowledgement of it. Simply smiling or saying 'thank you' will be enough for the other person to be sure that their compliment has been accepted. You may, at times, want to go further and say how you feel about your achievement. This need not imply arrogance but rather that you agree with what they are saying. For example: *'I'm glad you noticed. I was pleased with that report as well'*. Here you have also indicated that you are pleased that the other person has noticed that you have done something well. However, if you truly disagree with the praise, thank the giver before you qualify your response. *'Thank you for saying so. I'm not sure I agree with you. I think the section on management could be improved.'*

Positive Enquiry: Just as we use negative enquiry to clarify the nature of criticism (page 33) we can use positive enquiry to make sure that we truly understand praise we are given. On occasions, it is vague or exaggerated and so difficult to accept. Positive enquiry provides a means of questioning the person delivering the praise to help them to be more specific. Examples could include:

Patient: *'You nurses are so wonderful. I couldn't do what you do'*
Nurse: *'What makes you say that Mrs Smith?'*

or:

John: *'You're doing very well since you transferred to this department.'*
Sue: *'Thank you but in what particular ways do you think I'm doing well?'*
John: *'Well you've got a good telephone manner, you deal with callers very efficiently and ...'*
Sue: *Thank you John. That makes me feel good. I'm glad I transferred.'*

This approach will help you to accept compliments or praise more appropriately. The danger, at least in the early days of developing your assertion, is that you will feel even more self-conscious and embarrassed than before. Practice will make this easier since, with experience, you will be less worried about speaking out and expressing your appreciation of positive recognition of your work. Try doing this in role play with a partner until you feel more confident of your ability to both give and receive praise.

CHAPTER 7: SAYING NO (OR YES)

It is important to be able to say 'no'. The key to this is recognition that, although other people have the right to ask, you have the right to refuse. However, while saying 'no' may be appropriate, there are times when negotiation or compromise is the right or assertive thing to do. The important thing is that you have decided for yourself which action you wish to take.

REFUSING A REQUEST

Assertive techniques are often needed when we are being asked to do something against our wishes. We may feel we are being exploited or taken for granted.

Some people have little problem in saying 'no'; others find it difficult. How often do you hear the phrase *'I couldn't say no'*? Remember that you have the right to refuse any request, provided that you do so in a reasonable fashion. Being unreasonable or aggressive is likely to offend others and isolate you from them. What is needed then is a way of saying 'no' that does not damage your relationship with the person making the request. For non-assertive people this can be very difficult for many reasons so that we may agree to things that we would much rather refuse (Table 7.1).

Table 7.1   Some reasons why is it difficult to say 'no'

• Saying 'no' is selfish	• They won't like me if I refuse
• Its rude or aggressive	
• Others may feel hurt or rejected	• Their needs are more important than mine
• I feel sorry for them	• They may not ask again
• I'll feel guilty if I say 'no'	• I have no right to refuse
• There's no-one else	

The assertive way of saying no

The techniques used to refuse requests often combine a number of skills including:

- The 'broken record' (or 'instant replay')
- Appropriate body language
- Reflective listening
- Fogging
- Negative assertion

Six points should be remembered when saying 'no' (Figure 7.1).

Figure 7.1:   **Steps in the process of saying 'no'**

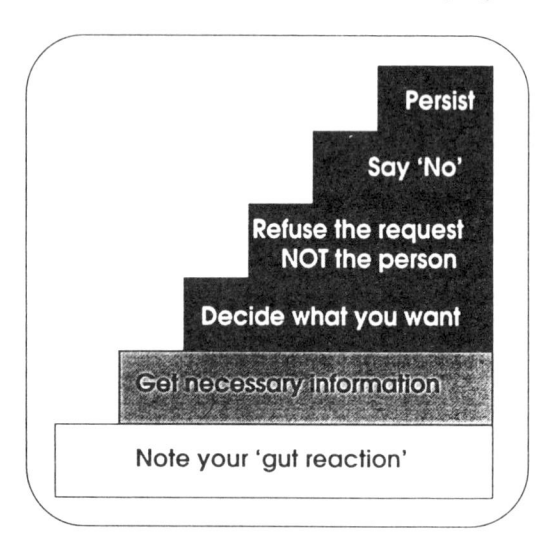

- Persist
- Say 'No'
- Refuse the request NOT the person
- Decide what you want
- Get necessary information
- Note your 'gut reaction'

'Gut reactions' are important. Your body often tells you how you feel, even before you have tried to respond. If you get that 'sinking feeling' then it usually means that you're reluctant and don't want to comply. Alternatively, you may want to respond wholeheartedly to the opportunity you have been offered and you're sure that you want to say 'yes'. Your gut reaction is often a good guide to what you really want rather than what you think you ought to do.

The difficulty arises when your feelings are less clear. Don't allow yourself to be forced into making a hasty decision. If you find you are hesitating - even a little - remember that saying 'yes' when you want to say 'no' can make you feel used, resentful, powerless and angry. Give yourself time to think. Move to the next step and ensure that you have all the information you need before making a decision.

Using a simple phrase, like *'I need to think about it'* may be enough to prevent you answering before you have thought it through. Other examples include: *'When would you want the report completed?'* or *'For how long would you want me to work in Joe's department?'*.

However, although asking questions may tell you what you need to know it may also cause surprise. People often become defensive if questioned, particularly if they were expecting you to agree. This forces them to think through their request from your perspective. Keep calm and persist in your request for information. Having obtained it you can then make your decision.

If you decide to say 'no', say so confidently and clearly. Use a short, clear statement that shows that you are turning down the request. Include the word 'no' so that there is no misunderstanding. As many of the problems associated with saying 'no' stem from guilt about letting others down or hurting their feelings we often feel we must explain our refusal. It is worth asking whether you are explaining because you want them to know why you feel unable to agree or if it is a way of hiding your anxiety about refusing. In other words, are you protecting yourself or the other person? Alternatively, we may give an excuse (rather than the real reason) to avoid upsetting someone or indicating disagreement with a particular action.

There are times when a brief 'no' is entirely appropriate, for example when others are trying to manipulate you or playing on your values (like friendship) or emotions (e.g. crying or becoming angry). A brief response, and persisting in your refusal, is the most effective way of dealing with this. However, when you *want* to explain or give a reason for your refusal, make sure this is genuine. Are you *really* sorry that you can't help? Remember, honesty is central to assertion! Keep any explanation short and to the point and, having given your reason, do not feel the need to justify it. Stick to the point and don't allow yourself to be pushed to justify your decision. For example:

Jenny: *'John, will you change your day off? I want to go out with my mother tomorrow.'*
John: *'No. I don't want to change my day off.'*
Jenny: *'Why not? You haven't got anything planned for tomorrow, you said so at coffee time. And my mother's looking forward to it.'*
John: *'I understand that your mother is looking forward to it but I don't*

>   *want to change my day off.'*
> Jenny: *'Why not? My mother's really looking forward to it.'*
> John: *'I've made my decision. I don't want to change my day off.'*
> Jenny: *'Oh. All right I'll ask Mary instead.'*

Here John has stuck to his decision and has not allowed Jenny to push him into explaining it. He has repeated his refusal, firmly and politely and has made good use of the broken record (see below). He has also taken responsibility for his action using 'I' statements to declare that he does not want to change his day off.

It is important to take responsibility for your decision. You don't need to 'pass the buck'; its your decision, take responsibility for it. Remember though that you're not rejecting the person only turning down the request. Show that you have listened using *Tracking* (see below) which relies on phrases like *'I understand ...'*, or *I realise ...'*. Make sure your refusal is clear and unambiguous.

The broken record (also known as the Instant Replay)

The broken record is useful when we want to make a point without being side-tracked, 'talked round' or getting into arguments. Choose a short statement expressing what you want to say and, regardless of the argument, repeat your broken record. If used indiscriminately however, you will sound just like a broken record, stuck in a groove! A technique called *Tracking* can help to avoid this. Here, you acknowledge what the other person is saying and, having done so, return to your broken record. John has done this effectively when he says *'I understand that your mother is looking forward to it but I don't want to change my day off.'* Using the broken record, tracking and assertive body language will help you to get your point across.

Although continuing to refuse, you may perhaps propose an alternative. For example, John might have suggested that Jenny ask Mary to change her day off. You may be willing to accept the task at another time or you may know someone who would to do it now.

Sometimes we can be made to feel that refusal will damage our relationships. Here we can use the broken record with other assertive techniques while we persist in saying 'no'. Examples include:

- Self-disclosure: *'I'm sure I would feel much the same but I can't agree because I'm already over-committed.'*

- Giving free information: *'I realise this is inconvenient but I've already promised Mitch I would finish his work today.'*
- Fogging: *'You may well be right that I'm being selfish but I must stick to my arrangements.'*
- Negative assertion: *'You're right that I haven't done much to help so far but I must follow through on my arrangements.'.*

When emotion is used against us the best approach is that of reflective listening (page 18) which demonstrates that you're hearing the request and showing empathy. While defending your rights you are also showing that you recognise the other's rights. This may be enough to calm the situation and allow rational discussion to follow.

There are, of course, times, particularly at work, when we cannot refuse to take on a task or to attend a meeting. For example, our contract of employment may stipulate certain functions. We *can*, however, make our feelings clear and state any difficulties that the situation may cause us. It may be possible to negotiate an alternative course of action (see page 52).

EXERCISE:
Think of a situation in which you find it difficult to say 'no'.
- Why is it difficult? (e.g. I'll be letting them down).
- Confront this and ask whether this is really likely to happen and, if it does, is it really a problem?
- Examine your needs in the situation and the needs of the others involved.
- Consider which of the techniques available to help you to say 'no' would be the most helpful in this case.
- Practise the technique in role play with a partner and ask them to give you feedback on your 'performance'.

Tips for assertive refusal

- Keep your reply short and to the point
- Be straightforward. Use expressions such as *'I prefer not to ...'*, *'No. I'm not happy to do ...'* or *'No. I don't want to ...'*
- Take responsibility for your decision using 'I' statements
- Give the real reason for your refusal, don't invent excuses

- Acknowledge the request and thank them for asking you
  'Thank you, John, but I'd prefer not to take that on ...'
- Use assertive body language. Speak slowly and steadily and with warmth. This is particularly important when using short phrases that can sound abrupt.

SAYING 'YES'

Surprising as it may seem, saying 'yes' can also be difficult, particularly for those who suffer from low self-esteem. You may wonder why on earth anyone should ask you. Perhaps they feel sorry for you or are they just 'being nice'? You may worry that you are not 'up to the job' (Table 7.2). Again you may need additional information to help you to reach an appropriate decision. Once adequate information is available, take time to think through the situation and identify why you would find it difficult to accept. Clearly, 'they' think that you can do it, otherwise you would not have been asked. Examine your thoughts calmly and realistically; ask yourself if you want to take on the task and whether it creates any opportunities for you. Having done this, say 'yes', clearly and definitely.

Table 7.2   Some reasons why is it difficult to say 'yes'

- They may not really mean it
- I'm not sure if I really want it
- I don't deserve it
- I don't have enough information
- I can't do it
- I have no right to refuse

If you have decided to say 'yes', then you must now co-operate. When you agree to something it is essential that you ensure that you do, indeed, carry it through. You have made a contract and you must stick to it unless you clearly indicate that you have changed your mind or realise that you have made a mistake. In this case use your newly acquired assertion to help you to admit your mistake.

MAKING REQUESTS

Just as we find it difficult to accept or reject requests we may find it difficult to make requests of others. This may depend on who we are asking as it can be easier to ask a colleague for help than to approach your manager about a change in your responsibilities. Making requests is, however, an essential skill and, if you cannot do this assertively, you may find that you miss opportunities or cannot obtain essential resources. This may arise because asking for help is seen as a sign of weakness; making requests may be felt to be putting others under obligation to us. Alternatively we may believe that we have no right to ask or that, if people refuse, this reflects their dislike of us. If this describes you it is likely that you make requests tentatively or apologetically.

Alternatively we may behave aggressively when making requests, challenging others to refuse. This reflects a belief that others cannot say 'no' and should be pleased to have been asked!

Making requests assertively

Remember that, although others may refuse, you have the right to ask. There may, however, be some exceptions as contracts of employment often stipulate what people **must** do. Individuals do, however, retain the right to raise any difficulties that agreeing to the request may cause; they may also reject unreasonable requests.

Assertive requests are made in a straightforward and open fashion rather than making it difficult for the other to refuse. Be direct and to the point so that the nature of the request is clear and keep it short so that people neither become suspicious or impatient. Give a clear reason for the request but don't justify yourself or feel it necessary to 'sell' the request by playing on friendship or with insincere flattery or tempting promises (*If you do this I'll give you ...*'). Simply ask for what you want.

Respect the fact that others have the right to refuse your request, particularly if this is of a personal nature. Under such circumstances don't become persistent but accept their refusal with good grace. If the request is work-related, and therefore difficult for the person to refuse, respect their right to seek further information or clarification about what is wanted. If they are still unable to meet your request it may be necessary to examine why this is so and enter into negotiation or some form of joint problem-solving to overcome any difficulties.

NEGOTIATION AND COMPROMISE

In truth, much of our everyday life is devoted to negotiation and compromise. We often have to meet others half-way and reach decisions based not only on our needs and preferences but also on those of other people. We even negotiate over where or when to go out for a meal, where to go on holiday or what to watch on TV. All these situations require some degree of discussion before a decision can be reached. It is at work, however, that many negotiations come into sharper focus and may become the centre of disagreement.

Whatever the level of negotiation, most participants share the wish to reach agreement with minimal disruption and ill-feeling. The aim is to put forward an opinion, listen 'properly' to the views of others and reach an amicable agreement.

Assertive negotiation comprises a number of steps:

1. Clarify your ideal solution and decide how strongly you feel about this.
2. Decide what solution you would be willing to settle for and how strongly you feel about it. Make this clear to the others involved.
3. Establish their ideal solution and how strongly they feel about it.
4. Taking account of both ideal solutions, and the strength of feeling associated with them, decide whether it is appropriate to reveal your second preference.
5. Try to establish what second preference the other person would be willing to accept. Reveal what you would be willing to settle for (your bottom line) and how strongly you feel about it.
6. If possible establish agreement.
7. Stick to your bottom line if the other person tries to push you further. Use the broken record to help you achieve this.

In other words, before you enter into discussion about a contentious issue, decide what is negotiable and what is not. Having decided this, ensure that you stick to it; this is your bottom line. If possible, plan a mutually convenient time and place with your opposite number and meet in an unhurried and relaxed fashion. Such planning helps to control the temptation to rush into negotiation when you are angry or irritated and so that you present your case in a disorganised fashion.

Take time to present your argument clearly and concisely reminding the other person of any pertinent agreements or promises. An effective presentation helps to overcome many of the problems of negotiation by 'setting the scene' and ensuring that both parties are clear about the subject under discussion. Both sides must present their cases clearly if they hope to reach agreement.

The process of negotiation

In general, the harder the work involved in reaching agreement the more successful a negotiation is judged to have been. If one person gives in too readily the other may lose respect or may continue to feel disgruntled thinking that, if it was so easy to 'win', they could have obtained more than they did.

This means that the process of negotiation is important and must be seen to be worthwhile. In the main, negotiation involves a system of 'nibbling away' at each other's requests to reach a realistic and manageable agreement in a balanced series of 'trade offs'.

It is important to help your opposite number to agree to your main requests by giving in to some of your subsidiary aims. Any action that helps them to feel good about their decisions to go along with some of your requests will help to maintain good relationships for the future. If, however, you are sure that you are not willing to negotiate on a particular issue you can employ assertive techniques to help you. Just repeat the fact - firmly, politely and impersonally.

David: *'Susan, this is a real emergency. I must have this information for a meeting at 2.00 this afternoon'*

Susan: *'I'm sorry. I've promised Sam these figures by lunch time. I simply can't give you that information by 2.00.'*

David: *'But this is an emergency - I must have it.'*

Susan: *'I'll let you have it as soon as I can but I can't give it to you by 2.00pm.'*

David: *But Susan, if I don't have it Sheila will be after my blood, I'll*

Susan: *lose my job. Sam won't mind if his figures are late'.*
Susan: *'I'm sorry David, I do understand your problem but I still can't do it by 2.00.'*
David: *'Of course you can, you just won't. You just don't seem to understand - this is a real emergency.'*
Susan: *'I'll have it for you as soon as I can but I can't do it by 2.00. I could probably manage it by mid-afternoon, say about 3.30?'*
David: *'Oh, all right. I'll have to see if I can delay the meeting till 4.00.'*

Here Susan has identified what is not negotiable and has stuck to it. Her bottom line was that she could not provide the information by 2.00pm. She repeated this, calmly and firmly, again and again. She stuck to her bottom line and, like a broken record, simply repeated it. The broken record has shown its value yet again. The difficult part is deciding what you are prepared to negotiate about. Once you have done this the rest should follow 'naturally'!

REACHING AGREEMENT

The techniques described here can also be applied in attempts to seek agreement - which is, after all, only another form of negotiation. We have seen that assertiveness can be a strong tool for this purpose. If you are leading a team or a group, and seeking to reach agreement, the following tips may help:

- Always listen actively and demonstrate that you have heard what team members have said
- Show that you respect what they are saying
- Find out what others feel and let them know how and what you feel
- Don't confuse feelings with emotions
- Offer ideas or solutions, don't impose them
- Seek ideas from group members and build on them. This helps to create 'ownership' of the agreement
- Remember that a group or team trying to reach agreement should act as a group and not as individuals there simply to make up the numbers!

CHAPTER 8: DEALING WITH NON-ASSERTION IN OTHERS

Dealing with non-assertion in others may pose significant difficulty and often influences our behaviour. For example, others may challenge your decisions attempting to 'persuade' you to change your mind or, by making you feel guilty or sorry for them, causing you to rethink your plans. This 'emotional blackmail' can make it difficult to maintain your assertion. It is necessary, therefore, to consider how such situations can be handled assertively.

HANDLING AGGRESSION

Dealing with aggression can be difficult and may lead us to respond in a similar vein; such situations often leave us emotionally drained. Finding ways of dealing with aggression will help us to retain control of our behaviour the aim being to change the interaction from an angry and aggressive exchange to one in which assertion can dominate, issues can be dealt with and both parties feel satisfied with the outcome. Doing this successfully will also make it less likely that the person will behave aggressively towards you in the future.

The main way of dealing with such situations is to take a deep breath, and then use reflective listening (page 18) to allow you to maintain empathy with the other person while maintaining your position. This helps to 'free' the other person from their emotional reaction enabling them to respond logically. In doing this it is important to ensure that you reflect the content as well as the feeling of the other's aggression in order to demonstrate recognition of their feelings. This gives them the opportunity to modify any exaggeration (which often accompanies aggression) and offers them the chance to become more reasonable. For example:

Aggressor: *'You have no right to talk to me like that. I know what I'm doing.'*

You: *'You feel that I'm wrong to tell you about my concern because you are happy with what you are doing?'*

To be effective in defusing the situation and reduce the level of emotion a reflective response must be non-judgmental. Unless this is so your reaction will simply 'fuel' the argument. You must demonstrate your respect for the other person.

Table 8.1   Feelings which may accompany aggression

- Anger
- Embarrassment
- Guilt
- Frustration
- Fear or anxiety
- Hurt

and his or her views and feelings (assertive) but do not allow him to 'side-track' you; use the broken record to help you to 'stick to the point'. When a reflective response does not seem to be helpful try one of the techniques used for dealing with criticism to help you to maintain your position (e.g. fogging or negative assertion) before returning to your point.

When these approaches do not seem to be helping the situation it may be necessary to ask questions to clarify the precise nature of the problem. By demonstrating your interest in resolving the situation you may succeed in defusing the emotion. It is essential, of course, that you ask these questions assertively keeping your voice level and even. Speaking slowly may help to slow the pace of the interaction but make sure that you listen to the responses. This approach is particularly useful when aggression arises unexpectedly and clear understanding is crucial to successful resolution of the problem. Examples include:

'When did this happen Jane?'
'Can you give me examples?'
'So, have I got this right? What you are saying is ...?'
'Can I just check what you're saying?'

EXERCISE:
With a partner, practise making assertive responses to aggression and ask them to give you feedback about the way you do this. You can do this alone in which case practice making assertive responses to yourself until you feel confident about doing this.

Dealing with aggression can be difficult and demanding; practising these techniques can give you confidence in handling it. Remember that you have the right to be assertive. However, if it becomes clear that the other person is too angry to allow meaningful discussion to take place use the techniques described on page 34-38 to help you to deal with his anger. When all else fails, and the situation remains emotionally charged, leave the room. Say that you are leaving but offer to talk about the problem later. Alternatively, just leave. Don't feel that you must stick it out; this will achieve little and is unlikely to resolve the problem.

HANDLING PASSIVITY

Non-assertion may be manifested by tentative or apologetic behaviour or by a complete absence of response. Such people tend to sit at the back of meetings failing to contribute, even when 'pushed'. The problem is that you won't know why they're silent. Do they disagree with the decision that is made? Have they something worthwhile to contribute to the discussion? The only thing that you will know is that you don't know what they really think or feel. This form of 'silent non-assertion' can be very difficult to detect at the time unless you look carefully at the accompanying body language. For example, there may be a lack of eye contact, or a doubtful facial expression. The individual may be restless or apparently uncomfortable. An awareness of these signs will help you to plan how to deal with the situation.

In dealing with non-assertion your aim is to uncover the underlying difficulties. Remember that, although a passive person may not be violating your rights, in overlooking this and failing to act assertively you may be ignoring his or her needs and feelings thus violating *his* rights. Thus, to allow you to be assertive, you need to know what his underlying beliefs, feelings and attitudes are.

Again asking non-critical questions may help to clarify the nature of the problem. For example: *'You seem to be hesitating. What's the problem?'* The person may, of course, deny any problem so that you may need to take this further adding something like: *'Let's see if I can help.'*. This makes it clear that you realise that there is a difficulty and makes your willingness to address it apparent.

Table 8.2   Some feelings which may accompany passivity

- Helplessness and self pity
- Lack of confidence
- Self-criticism
- Feeling inferior to others
- Fear and anxiety

Take care to distinguish between genuine difficulties and excuses but, again, take care since making this evident may act as a 'red rag to a bull' making the other person think that you're accusing him of lying. For example:

Other person: *'I haven't done that report yet. I've been busy with x and I'm away for most of next week.'*

You: *'Oh, I see. Well, let's see how we can get it done.'*

You could follow this up the next week with something like: *'John, I'd like to have that report by the end of next week. Is that all right with you?'* Ensure that you get an answer to your question and, if necessary, use negotiation to help you to reach agreement.

Although it may be tempting to overlook passivity and 'let sleeping dogs lie' this is not desirable since, in the longer term, it may be disruptive when, for example, a lack of **disagreement** is mistaken for **agreement**. In this situation, you may find a passive individual is undermining your decisions by failing to follow agreed procedures. When questioned you may then find that they did not agree with the decision but, by failing to make this known, let you believe they were in agreement. Such situations may create significant problems if they are not dealt with effectively.

Sometimes, you may have to accept that it is simply not possible to gain an assertive response. Maintaining your assertion in the face of passivity may be the best you can achieve. On other occasions the individual may become irritated and act aggressively. This is particularly likely when he can see that he is not going to gain your sympathy or when he regards your questioning approach as threatening. If this occurs then you can maintain your assertion employing the techniques described in the previous section.

In all interactions with passive individuals maintain an assertive tone of voice and demonstrate empathy rather then criticism. Do not fall into the trap of demonstrating sympathy for him or for his problems. Some of us feel that we must always be caring, compassionate and attentive to others, even when we do not want to be. Feeling like this can prevent us from being assertive. This is not to say that assertive people are not compassionate just that they don't get caught in the 'compassion trap'; they set limits for themselves. Again reflective listening can be helpful here.

Reflective listening, as applied to dealing with non-assertion, has the effect of helping you to find out more about the other person and the relationship between you. In this way it helps to identify common ground making resolution much more likely. Although you are looking for a mutually acceptable solution to any particular problem a solution suggested by the other is more likely to be adhered to than one that is imposed. Thus, where possible, this should be achieved by negotiation that takes account of the needs of all involved. Following this a review period should be established for the agreed action to ensure that both parties have followed through.

Adopting the processes discussed in this chapter will help us to maintain our assertion in the face of non-assertion from others. If we persist in our approach, recognising both our own rights and those of the others involved, it should prove possible to achieve a solution which will, in turn, lead to improved relationships in the working environment.

CHAPTER 9: A PROGRAMME FOR CHANGE

By now you should have a clear idea of what assertiveness is and have decided that you would like to change at least some of your attitudes or behaviours and replace them with assertive characteristics. The next stage is to set yourself some goals and develop a plan of action to help you to work towards them. Keep a diary of the journey towards increasing your personal effectiveness.

However, there are some general points that you should consider before you go too far down this road.

Permission: We all require permission to change so give yourself permission to become assertive. To do this you must give yourself positive messages to encourage you and reinforce positive things about yourself and the way you feel. Whenever you feel your inner voice trying to say something negative, stop it and try to think of something positive about the same issue. Instead of using phrases like *'I'll try'* or *'I wish'* say *'I can'*, *'I will'* and *'I do'*. Use such statements to support your actions; although they may not actually be true at the moment, telling yourself is the first step to making them come true!

Developing positive affirmations: Start by making positive statements to yourself perhaps simple things like *'I am happy'*, *'I feel confident'*, *'I can do that'*. Say these things in the present tense emphasising their positive aspects.

> **EXERCISE: Developing positive affirmations.**
> Write a list of 10-12 things you like about yourself. These may reflect your skills, abilities, qualities, achievements or any other aspect of yourself.
> Use this list to help you to write a number of positive statements about yourself. Read it to yourself every day; add to it when you think of other achievements or successes.

Once you have developed the habit of using simple positive statements to support and boost your self-esteem, move on giving yourself stronger messages, show that you appreciate yourself; the more we appreciate ourselves the less we depend on others for our self-esteem. Use the exercise above to help you to do this.

Some examples of positive affirmations include:

> *'I can do anything I want to do'*
> *'I am capable of making my own decisions'*
> *'I can determine what happens to me'.*

Another important step in supporting your decision to become assertive, and to emphasise that you have your permission to do so, is to visualise yourself as you are going to be. Actually see yourself performing assertively, imagine how you will feel when you do this successfully. Think about it carefully using your positive affirmations to help; see your new image in great detail and go over it until it is a familiar to you as your current self. Imagine yourself in situations where you are being assertive. *Feel* confident, capable, powerful. *Hear* your voice sounding strong and steady. *Hear* the words you are using. *Experience* the satisfaction of being assertive. This will reinforce your picture of yourself as an assertive person and help you on the road to becoming what you want to become. When you can do this successfully you have begun to become an assertive person!

Be realistic: Make sure that you set yourself realistic goals (i.e. goals that are achievable and possible). If they are not you are setting yourself up to fail. This can become a self-fulfilling prophecy, a phenomenon which often arises without our conscious awareness of it and causes us to experience that which we expect to experience (i.e. we often succeed or fail because we subconsciously *knew* that we would). This shows how our expectations and attitudes can exert a powerful influence on the outcome.

To create positive outcomes you must start with positive expectations. In other words, *use* the power of self-fulfilling prophecy to help you to create positive experiences. This is where positive affirmations can help but, even when using these, we may 'sabotage' our efforts by setting unrealistic goals! Set yourself small steps, or larger goals that can be broken down into smaller parts, which can be achieved one at a time.

None of us can change the habits or behaviours of a lifetime overnight; it takes time and we should be aiming to make slow steady progress rather than achieving an instant 'miracle cure'!

Don't be tempted to take on too much at a time, take things slowly and gradually build on your success. Don't label yourself a 'failure' simply because you don't succeed all the time; your *attempt* at assertion may have been less successful than you had hoped but this does not make *you* a failure. It should instead act as a spur to drive you on! None of us can 'get it right' all the time. Remember that we're all allowed to make mistakes.

Because you're trying new or modified behaviours in handling particular situations you may be unsuccessful in a number of ways:

- You may fail to maintain your assertion
- You may not achieve the desired objective
- The other person may not accept your right to be assertive.

In all these cases, reflecting on the situation will help you to see what went well and what went badly and how you could change your behaviour so that, if the situation were to arise again, you could alter the outcome. Make notes on your reflections in your diary. Do not downplay your successes or exaggerate your failures. Instead try to be honest so that you can analyse what happened rationally and learn from it. Unless you do this you will not gain an objective view or a basis for further evaluation. The framework shown in Figure 9.1 may help you to achieve this.

Look back at your reflections from time to time and evaluate your progress. Were your goals realistic? Remember that people lacking confidence are experts at setting unrealistic goals so don't be surprised if, when reviewing your goals, you find you were expecting too much of yourself.

Establishing goals: It is often easier to set long-term goals than to establish short-term ones so that it may be easier to set those goals that are furthest away and work backwards from them - say 1 year, 6 months, 3 months, 1 month and so on. Make your goals clear and specific; if they're vague you will never be sure whether you have really achieved them! Make positive statements which affirm your intentions. For example, not *'I want to ...'* but *'I will ...'*. Also give each a time scale and target date for achievement.

Figure 9.1   A framework for reflection

Situation/event	Describe the situation as it occurred (i.e. what happened?)
Contributory factors	What factors contributed to the way the situation developed?
Context	Were there any relevant background factors that may have influenced the way the event developed?
Reflection	Consider: What you were trying to achieve Why you acted in the way that you did? How you felt at the time. How did the other person feel? What factors do you think influenced your behaviour?
Alternative actions	Could you have behaved in another way? What would the consequences have been had you handled the situation differently?
Learning	How do you feel about the experience? Could you have dealt with it better? What you have learned?

Focusing on your goal(s) helps to concentrate your thoughts on achievement rather than on the obstacles or problems you imagine getting in the way. In addition, if you are remain aware of your goals, you will also remain aware of the steps that you need to take to achieve the desired result. You will then be able to choose what actions to take to help you to meet your ultimate goal(s).

Remember, if your goals are realistic they will be achievable; if they are achievable you will reach them. This will encourage you to move to the next step.

Practice: Whether you are learning to ride a bicycle, make a cake, knit a jumper or develop and use assertive behaviour it takes more than 'simple' understanding of the underlying concepts and principles involved. You must also try them out. To become skilled at any task requires practice and, remember that, when you're practising, you don't have to be perfect, you're allowed to make mistakes! How often did you fall off your bicycle before you learned to ride it? How many stitches did you drop when you knitted that first jumper? So it is with assertiveness. A dropped stitch or a fall from the saddle didn't stop you from trying again; why should it do so now?

If you have decided that you want to become more assertive then practice is essential. Indeed, a great deal of practice may be needed to become skilful in any new behaviour before it becomes a 'natural' part of you.

So what can you do to increase your chances of success? The following steps should help you to begin to integrate assertiveness into your natural behaviour.

- Selecting the right situation
- Appropriate preparation
- Adopting assertive behaviour in specific situations
- Reflecting on the outcome.

Choose your situation carefully: Be selective about when and where you choose to start developing your assertiveness. Remember that behavioural change takes place in stages; start with small problems in relatively 'safe' situations where you think there is a reasonably good chance of success. When trying to choose appropriate times consider the advantages and disadvantages that may follow your increased assertion; ideally you are seeking situations where the benefits clearly outweigh any negative consequences. For example don't start by asking for a rise if it means you may hear something you don't want to hear about your performance. On the other hand, if you feel relatively secure at work, attempting smaller changes may be the places for you to start. Change one thing at a time so that you don't become overwhelmed. The exercise that follows may help you to identify appropriate situations.

> **EXERCISE:**
> Think of a situation at work when you behave non-assertively. What are the benefits for you in behaving in the way you do? What are the disadvantages for you in behaving in this way? Identify what you may gain by being assertive in this situation. Consider, for example, the following: self-respect, being true to yourself, developing honest relationships or clear and unambiguous communication. But don't restrict yourself to these factors, be honest and examine the situation carefully.
> What, if anything, have you got to lose in this situation?
> Having explored the issue thoroughly make an informed choice - do you want to learn to be assertive in this situation?
> Record your responses.

Preparation: Effective and thorough preparation is essential for your first attempts at developing assertive communication. Working through the following steps beforehand may help to increase the likelihood of success:

- Clarify your objective - what do you want to achieve?
- Clarify both your rights and those of the other person - plan how to recognise these and demonstrate that you are doing so
- Use positive affirmations to support and reinforce your intentions (*'I can ...'*, *'I will ...'*)
- Use visualisation to help you to 'see' yourself performing successfully
- Planning the assertive statements that you will use to start the interaction.

In the early stages, you may find it helpful to jot down some notes under each of these headings to help you to clarify what you intend to do. Use the framework given in Figure 9.2 to help you. Practise saying the actual words you will use in the appropriate tone of voice. This should help you to start the interaction assertively; if you start off badly, by being aggressive or apologetic, for example, it can be difficult to regain your momentum.

Figure 9.2 A suggested framework for preparation for an assertive interaction

	Notes
Situation in which I wish to be assertive	
Objective (what I want to achieve)	
My rights (relevant to this situation)	
The other person's rights in this situation	
Positive affirmations	
Initial assertive statement	

It can also be helpful to consider how you will respond should the other person react in an unexpected way or fail to accept your assertion. Remember though that assertion will not solve all your problems or ensure that you always get what you want. What it will do is ensure that you make your needs clear and enable negotiation to take place. It will also help you to feel good about yourself and to believe that you have handled the situation effectively. You will have taken responsibility for your feelings and made them clear to the other person. At the same time, although you have made your feelings clear, you will not have damaged your relationship with the person concerned; your self esteem will be intact. This will reinforce your action making it easier next time.

In this way careful planning can help to achieve a successful outcome. Reflecting on the situation will help you to identify the strengths and weaknesses of your approach, improving your confidence. Later, when you have gained in confidence, you can dispense with your notes simply thinking situations through and clarifying your intended actions in your mind. With time you will need less and less time for planning; assertion will become integrated into your usual (or 'normal') behaviour adding another skill to your existing repertoire.

Adopting and maintaining your assertion: If you have prepared thoroughly you should be reasonably confident that you can deal with the situation effectively. If you use your assertive opening statement as planned this will give you a good start. If the person responds as you expect all well and good, you are prepared and able to deal with his or her responses. But if the response is truly unexpected, buy some time to enable you to think of an assertive response - it is surprising how quickly you can do this once you have thought it through (probably less than half a second!). This can be achieved in a number of ways. For example:

- Responsive assertions which seek clarification or ensure that you have fully understood what has been said (e.g. *'Can I clarify this...?' Do you mean ....?' 'Are you saying....?'*)
- Assertively taking 'time out' (e.g. *'I'd like a minute to think about this'*).

Once the encounter is over, reflect on your 'performance'. This may not be possible immediately so take care not to let any 'problems' build so that they seem insurmountable. Be realistic and review the situation objectively as described here.

Reflecting on the outcome: The importance of reflection has been stressed throughout this chapter for the simple reason that it is vital to continuing development. A rational analysis can allow you to learn from each event. When appropriate congratulate yourself - you deserve it! When an encounter did not go as you planned, sound reflection will help you to work out improved responses to predictable situations. It will also encourage you to start working on other areas of your assertiveness which you feel would benefit from improvement.

Unexpected situations: Unexpected situations do, of course, sometimes arise. By their very nature they are unexpected and so cannot be predicted or prepared for in advance (e.g. a subordinate verbally attacks you). In the early stages of developing your assertion skills such events can be very demanding and an apparent inability to respond assertively can knock your confidence. It is particularly important that you are realistic when reviewing your performance in such situations - it is very easy to become discouraged. Remember that the event was unexpected, you didn't have time to prepare. It is easy to be critical. Instead, look at the situation as objectively as possible and think about how you might respond better should it arise again.

FINAL TIPS

Be patient: Changing the habits of a lifetime can't be achieved overnight.

Be persistent: There will be times when you feel discouraged and dissatisfied with your progress. This is natural and it is worth sitting back and reviewing your progress to date. Read through your diary and study your reflections to help you to consolidate what you have already learned; congratulate yourself on your achievements so far. If you are trying to work alone this may be the time to seek some support from friends, family or colleagues. Remember that successful people know how important it is to be prepared to ask for help and support from others.

Enjoy yourself: You choose to develop your assertiveness, it is a voyage of discovery helping you to become more aware of yourself, your beliefs and feelings while, at the same time, recognising that others have the right to do the same. It should not feel heavy and onerous although it may, at times, be a little painful since exploring your feelings can be difficult. It is also exciting to learn more about yourself. Developing your skills should be stimulating and interesting. To support yourself through the difficult times make sure that you can give yourself plenty of treats and rewards for 'good behaviour'!

Don't compare yourself to anyone else: You are an individual; this makes you different from anyone else and means that your beliefs and feelings will also be different. Your progress towards assertion will depend on an infinite number of factors many of which are unique to you. This means that the only evaluation you need is that which is based on a comparison of your current performance with that which you exhibited when you first started your development programme. Use your diary to help you to progress.

Don't allow others to evaluate your progress: As your behaviour changes others may be disconcerted by the 'new' you. If you were previously a passive person they will be surprised when you use

Table 9.1   A programme for change

- Give yourself permission to change:
    Positive affirmation
    Positive visualisation
- Be realistic:
    Achievable goals
    Use the power of self-fulfilling prophecy
- Practice and reflect; evaluate changes
- Patience is a virtue!
- Persistence is essential
- Have fun - self-discovery is enjoyable
- Don't compare yourself with others; self-development is an individual pursuit.

assertive techniques to make your feelings known. If you were previously aggressive, they may heave a sigh of relief! But, in the end, only you can judge your behaviour and feelings. Remember that successful change depends on knowing what you want and being able to judge when you've achieved it.

Of course, you can want and need support encouragement and constructive feedback; you do *not* want judgement from friends and colleagues. The only judgement you should allow is from those such as your employer who may have specific expectation of your performance and require confident (and assertive) behaviour. This may, for example, be discussed in an appraisal interview.

But, in the end, don't forget that your ultimate aim is not only to appear confident and assertive but also to *feel* confident and assertive. Only you can judge whether you have achieved this. Its a voyage of discovery - enjoy it - and good luck!

REFERENCES

Berne, E., 1967, *Games People Play*, Penguin, London.

Back K., and Back, K., 1982, *Assertiveness at Work* (second edition), McGraw-Hill Book Company, London.

Dickson, A., 1982, *A Woman in Your Own Right*, Quartet Books, London.

Gournay, K., 1995, *Stress Management: a Guide to Coping with Stress*, Asset Books, Leatherhead.

Pease, A., 1981, *Body Language. How to Read Others' Thoughts by their Gestures*, Sheldon Press, London.

Sharpe, R., 1984, *Assert Yourself. How to do a Good Deal Better with Others* (second edition), Kogan Page, London

Townend, A., 1991, *Developing Assertiveness*, Routledge, London.

FURTHER READING

Alberti, R. E. and Emmons M. L., 1986, *Your Perfect Right. A Guide to Assertive Living*, Impact Publishers, California.

Cox, G. and Dainow, S., 1985, *Making the Most of Yourself*, Sheldon Press, London.

Mulhall, A., 1995, *Your Problem or Mine? A Guide to Handling 'Difficult People'*, Asset Books, Leatherhead.

Le Poole, S., 1987, *Never Take No for an Answer. A Guide to Successful Negotiation*, Kogan Page, London.

Lindenfield, G., *Managing Anger. Positive Strategies for Dealing with Difficult Emotions*, Thorsons, London.

Lindenfield, G., *Self Esteem*, Thorsons, London.

Pease, A., 1981, *Body Language. How to Read Others' Thoughts by their Gestures*, Sheldon Press, London.